PEOPLE TRIVIA!

Uncover a stash of tantalizing celebrity trivia. They're all here, from Brooke Shields to Frank Sinatra, from Robert Redford to Phil Donahue. They're the big, the bold, the bad, and the beautiful—and they're all in TRIVIA MANIA. Make yourself famous as a trivia star right now by trying these celebrity stumpers:

—Joanne Woodward is Paul Newman's first wife. True or false?
—What actor/comedian made "noogies" famous?
—Was Rock Hudson ever married?
—What was the name of the Lindberghs' baby?
—Who was with Nelson Rockefeller when he died?
—What star of *Taxi* is married to a star of *Cheers*?
—One-time music star Cat Stevens is now a penniless beggar in what foreign country?
—What famous member of a comedy team smuggled secret papers out of Russia?
—What gangster coined the expression "G-men" to describe FBI agents?
—Tom Parker, Elvis Presley's manager, is known by what title?

For the answers to these and a thousand other fascinating questions, keep on reading and surrender yourself to TRIVIA MANIA!

PEOPLE

TRIVIA Mania

BY XAVIER EINSTEIN

ZEBRA BOOKS
KENSINGTON PUBLISHING CORP.

Q) Who has a (non-trivial) mania for theatre, movies and Chinese food—and without whom it would have been literally *impossible for me to write this book?*

A) Barbara Teich

ZEBRA BOOKS

are published by

Kensington Publishing Corp.
475 Park Avenue South
New York, N.Y. 10016

First printing: August, 1984

Printed in the United States of America

TRIVIA MANIA:
People

1) Which of the following Hollywood couples did *not* marry and divorce each other twice?
   a. Richard Burton and Elizabeth Taylor
   b. Robert Wagner and Natalie Wood
   c. George C. Scott and Colleen Dewhurst
   d. George Peppard and Elizabeth Ashley

2) What star of the soap opera *All My Children* is rumored to be the highest-paid actress on daytime television?

3) Classy Fred Astaire went off to the races and married a female jockey. What is her name?

4) Clint Eastwood is married to his regular leading lady, Sondra Locke. True or false?

5) What lawyer won the largest divorce settlement ($85 million) in U.S. history for Sheika Dena Al-Farri?

6) Bruce Jenner, Olympic medal winner and T.V. personality, divorced his first wife to marry Elvis Presley's former girlfriend. What was her name?

. . . *Answers*

1. b (At the time of Natalie's untimely death they had been married twice and divorced once.)

2. Susan Lucci (who plays Erica)

3. Robyn Smith

4. false

5. Marvin Mitchelson

6. Linda Thompson

QUESTIONS

7) Actor Burt Reynolds has *not* been romantically linked with which of the following famous women?
   a. Dinah Shore
   b. Sally Field
   c. Suzanne Somers
   d. Loni Anderson

8) Who was the bandleader mentor of Ella Fitzgerald with whom she cowrote "A-Tisket, A-Tasket"?

9) Wally Amos is famous for what sweet success?

10) Gary Dahl invented a humor phenomenon that swept the nation a decade ago. What was it?

11) Who was the most recent little girl to grow up in the White House?

12) Who was responsible for starting the tax-revolt movement in 1978 with Proposition 13 in California?

13) Dale Evans married Roy Rogers long before they made movies together. True or false?

14) What erstwhile revolutionary was known as "Tanya" in the mid 1970s?

15) She's known as both "The Iron Lady" and "Attila the Hen." Who is she?

16) Spartacus is only a fictional character. True or false?

. . . *Answers*

7. c

8. Chick Webb

9. Famous Amos Chocolate Chip Cookies

10. The Pet Rock

11. Amy Carter

12. Howard Jarvis

13. False

14. Patty Hearst

15. Margaret Thatcher, Prime Minister of England

16. False (He died in 71 B.C.)

17) Stanley Applebaum is the real name of:
   a. Robert Vaughn
   b. Steve Lawrence
   c. Robert Goulet
   d. Tony Roberts

18) Actress Pam Grier (*Fort Apache, The Bronx*) and former football star, now actor, Roosevelt (Rosie) Grier are cousins. True or false?

19) Up-and-coming model/actress Kelly Collins is the beautiful kid sister of what modern-day sex symbol?

20) Who is the first and only woman to sit on the U.S. Supreme Court?

21) What is the name of the one-time Soviet ambassador to the U.S. and present Russian foreign minister who has negotiated with nine U.S. presidents?

22) To what famous actress was movie producer David O. Selznick married?

23) Howard L. Hunt, the incredibly wealthy Texas oil man, consulted a fortune teller before making important business deals. True or false?

24) What university does Jennifer Beals (*Flashdance*) attend?
   a. Yale
   b. Princeton
   c. Vassar
   d. Columbia

. . . Answers

17. c

18. True

19. Bo Derek

20. Sandra Day O'Connor

21. Andrei Gromyko

22. Jennifer Jones

23. True

24. a

25) What is the name of the late Karen Carpenter's performing brother?

26) Actress Diana Dors was once married to what actor/comedian who has since become a well-known TV game-show host?

27) Singing star Lionel Richie came out of what rock group?

28) Actress Melissa Gilbert (*Little House on the Prairie*) is having a well-publicized romance with what young actor?

29) Who is the present Secretary-General of the United Nations and what is his nationality?

30) Where was Bob Hope born?

31) Who took over as conductor of the Boston Pops after Arthur Fiedler's long reign?

32) TV actor/comedian Gabe Kaplan is a very serious gambler who plays what game for very high stakes?

33) Jane Fonda, while portraying a call girl in a hit movie, had close relations with what costarring actor?

34) Who was "The Naked Civil Servant"?

35) Which of the following is a famous culinary critic?
    a. Clive Revill
    b. Ross Claiborne
    c. Craig Claiborne
    d. Craig Wasson

. . . Answers

25. Richard Carpenter

26. Richard Dawson (*Family Feud*)

27. The Commodores

28. Rob Lowe

29. Javier Perez de Cuellar, a Peruvian

30. England

31. John Williams

32. Poker

33. Donald Sutherland

34. Quentin Crisp

35. c

36) Ron Wood is a member of The Beach Boys. True or false?

37) Stefano Casiraghi is married to what European celebrity?

38) Who was "The Smiling Pope"?

39) Who is TV- and motion-picture star Kristy McNichol's show-biz brother?

40) To what city was famous Russian dissident Andrei Sakharov banished?

41) Jack the Ripper was probably, in real life, a man called Ivor Novello. True or false?

42) Who is the burly one-time professional football player who became a popular folk singer and successful actor?

43) Former comedian Marty Ingels and his wife Shirley Jones successfully sued what publication?

44) James Dean died in a motorcycle accident. True or false?

45) Movie director Michael Curtiz, producer Alexander Korda, and actor Bela Lugosi all came from what country in Europe?

46) Who built and flew the "Spruce Goose"?

47) Of what discipline was the famous western gunman, Doc Holiday, a doctor?

. . . Answers

36. False (The Rolling Stones)

37. Princess Caroline of Monaco

38. John Paul I

39. Jimmy McNichol

40. Gorky

41. False (Ivor Novello played the Ripper in an early 1930s movie. No one knows who the Ripper really was.)

42. Burl Ives

43. *The National Enquirer*

44. False (car accident)

45. Hungary

46. Howard Hughes

47. Dentistry

QUESTIONS

48) TV actor David Hedison (*Voyage To The Bottom Of The Sea*) had a different stage name at one point in his career. What was it?

49) What were the first names of comedians Olsen and Johnson?

50) In the late 1970s a former Miss Wyoming was accused of kidnapping and raping a male Mormon missionary in England. True or false?

51) What sterling star of Hollywood (who appeared in *Dr. Strangelove*) has also been a famous sailor and a successful novelist?

52) Who is actress Goldie Hawn's current actor boyfriend?

53) Former Attorney General John Mitchell was accused and acquitted on a charge of conspiracy. True or false?

54) Who was President Lyndon Johnson's press secretary?
   a. Ron Nessen
   b. Pierre Salinger
   c. Bill Moyers
   d. Peter Jennings

55) What famous British actor lost his voice after an operation in 1966?

56) Who was actress June Havoc's legendary sister?

57) Lauren Bacall has been romantically linked with what actor who co-starred with her in Broadway's *Applause*?

... Answers

48. Al Hedison

49. Ole Olsen and Chic Johnson

50. True

51. Sterling Hayden

52. Kurt Russell

53. True (He was later convicted of perjury.)

54. c

55. Jack Hawkins

56. Gypsy Rose Lee

57. Harry Guardino

58) Who was playwright George S. Kaufman's best-known collaborator?

59) The name Neal Cassady is associated with:
    a. the Beat Generation
    b. Broadway
    c. bubblegum music
    d. The Jazz Age

60) Billie Jean King and her husband, Larry, are the parents of two children, both girls. True or false?

61) Who was the young evangelist who became an actor after a successful documentary was made about his life?

62) Friedrich Anton Mesmer introduced the use of hypnotism in medicine. True or false?

63) What famous singer wrote a biography of Judy Garland called *The Other Side of the Rainbow*?

64) The first woman pilot to fly for a major airline was:
    a. Jenny Carstairs
    b. Betty Kincaid
    c. Bonnie Tiburzi
    d. Leslie Jackson

65) What world-renowned bridge player is also an internationally famous movie star?

66) Famed sex researchers Masters and Johnson are married to each other. True or false?

. . . *Answers*

58. Moss Hart

59. a

60. False (They have no children.)

61. Marjoe Gortner

62. True

63. Mel Torme

64. c

65. Omar Sharif

66. True

67) What was the name of the woman who died at Chappaquiddick?

68) From what English university did Prince Charles graduate?

69) Who was the lawyer who defended The Boston Strangler and Dr. Sam Sheppard?
   a. Melvin Belli
   b. Roy Cohn
   c. F. Lee Bailey
   d. Louis Nizer

70) What is the real name of gossip columnist Suzy?

71) Who is Mia Farrow's mother?

72) Who were the four famous founders of United Artists?

73) Ellery Queen is really two people. Who are they?

74) This red-headed former model starred in *My Wild Irish Rose* and dozens of other films, but she's probably known best today as a beauty expert. Who is she?

75) Who is the surrealist painter who collaborated on two famous films with director Luis Buñuel?

76) Frank Sinatra started the "Rat Pack." True or false?

77) Joseph Cotton, who played a drama critic in his movie debut (*Citizen Kane*), had actually once been a drama critic in real life. True or false?

. . . Answers

67. Mary Jo Kopechne

68. Cambridge

69. c

70. Aileen Mehle

71. Maureen O'Sullivan

72. Douglas Fairbanks, Mary Pickford, Charles Chaplin, and D.W. Griffith

73. Frederick Dannay and Manfred Lee

74. Arlene Dahl

75. Salvador Dali

76. False (Humphrey Bogart did.)

77. True

78) By what other name was prison inmate Robert Stroud known?

79) Who is the husband of legendary theater star Jessica Tandy and her costar in the critically acclaimed *The Gin Game*?

80) Aaron Burr and Alexander Hamilton fought a duel. Which one of them lost and died?

81) Who was George McGovern's *first* vice-presidential running mate in the 1972 national election campaign?

82) The "Simon" of the publishing company Simon & Schuster is the father of:
   a. Paul Simon
   b. Carly Simon
   c. William Simon
   d. Neil Simon

83) What was Buffalo Bill's real name?

84) Carlotta Monti was the mistress of what famous comedian? (Hint: she wrote a book about their relationship that was later turned into a movie.)

85) Who was the woman involved in England's famous Profumo scandal?

86) Errol Flynn was born in Australia. True or false?

87) What well-known TV talk show host was a lay preacher by the time he was seventeen?

. . . *Answers*

78. The Birdman of Alcatraz

79. Hume Cronyn

80. Alexander Hamilton

81. Senator Thomas F. Eagleton of Missouri

82. b

83. William Cody

84. W.C. Fields

85. Christine Keeler

86. False (He was born in Tasmania.)

87. David Frost

88) From what state did Senator Margaret Chase Smith come?

89) Who has dedicated his life to hunting down Nazi war criminals?

90) What two historical figures, who fought each other in a famous battle, each have a food named after them?

91) Where did gangster John Dillinger die?

92) What was silent film comedian "Fatty" Arbuckle's real first name?

93) Which of the following is *not* one of Michael Jackson's siblings?
    a. Jackie
    b. Maureen
    c. Janet
    d. Gary

94) Ballet dancer Aleksandr Godunov has been involved with what movie star for the last three years?

95) Herbert Hoover was a mining engineer who had worked in Australia and China before eventually becoming President. True or false?

96) What famous actress made her first appearance on stage at the age of five in the year 1901 as "Baby _____"?

97) What was the name of the company that the real Karen Silkwood worked for at the time of her death?

. . . Answers

88. Maine

89. Simon Wiesenthal

90. Napoleon (the pastry) and (Beef) Wellington

91. Coming out of a Chicago movie theater

92. Roscoe

93. d

94. Jacqueline Bisset

95. True

96. Lillian (Gish)

97. Kerr-McGee

98) Who is the lead vocalist for the English rock group Duran Duran?

99) Which of the following actresses is the daughter of Sir Winston Churchill?

   a. Diana Churchill
   b. Marguerite Churchill
   c. Sarah Churchill
   d. all of the above

100) Charles Aznavour was born in:
   a. Armenia
   b. Paris
   c. Quebec
   d. Corsica

101) What remarkable coincidence occurred on July 4, 1826, the 50th anniversary of the signing of The Declaration of Independence?

102) What is the name of Caroline Kennedy's middle-aged boyfriend?

103) Who is the current director of the FBI?

104) Dashiell Hammett, who created the characters of Sam Spade and The Thin Man, was himself a detective. True or false?

105) Who was John Lennon's secretary and lover during his marriage to Yoko Ono?

. . . Answers

98. Simon Le Bon

99. c

100. a

101. Both John Adams and Thomas Jefferson died.

102. Edwin Schlossberg

103. William Webster

104. True

105. May Pang

106) What Oscar-winning American actor began his show-business career as a circus acrobat?

107) Prince Andrew of England was reportedly involved with what star of soft-porn movies?

108) Sting, lead singer of The Police, once earned his living as a:
    a. bartender
    b. teacher
    c. policeman
    d. hairdresser

109) The *New York Times* slogan "All The News That's Fit To Print" was created by what publisher?

110) Who is the actress daughter of the famous founder of "The New York Actor's Studio"?

111) What legendary American folksinger was "bound for a glory all his own"?

112) What was the maiden name of the 26-year-old American woman who became Queen of Jordan when she married King Hussein in 1978?

113) Eve Arden, who starred as *Our Miss Brooks* on TV, performed with the Ziegfeld Follies. True or false?

114) Eva Peron, the subject of the hit Broadway musical *Evita*, was the wife of what ruler of Argentina?

115) What former Harvard professor is most closely associated with the counter culture of the 1960s?

. . . *Answers*

106. Burt Lancaster

107. Koo Stark

108. b

109. Adolph Ochs

110. Susan Strasberg

111. Woody Guthrie

112. Elizabeth Halaby

113. True

114. Juan Peron

115. Timothy Leary

16) What well-known former CIA operative claimed that as a child he roasted a rat and ate it to overcome his fear of rodents?

117) Teddy Roosevelt founded and led what military group?

118) Who is called "The Philosopher of Pessimism"?
   a. Jung
   b. Descartes
   c. Schopenhauer
   d. Spinoza

119) Who was with Nelson Rockefeller when he died?

120) Actress Susan Sarandon and actor Chris Sarandon are brother and sister. True or false?

121) Who was the social secretary that Eleanor Roosevelt hired for FDR, who later had an affair with the President?

122) What was the name of Claus Von Bulow's lover who testified for the prosecution in his 1982 trial?

123) Who was America's "Sweater Girl"?

124) What was the real name of writer Ross Macdonald, creator of the hero Lew Archer?

125) Who was Woody Allen's first wife?
   a. Louise Lasser
   b. Carol Fishbein
   c. Dianne Keaton
   d. Harlene Rosen

. . . *Answers*

116. G. Gordon Liddy

117. The Rough Riders

118. c

119. Megan Marshack

120. False (They were married.)

121. Lucy Mercer

122. Alexandra Isles

123. Lana Turner

124. Kenneth Millar

125. d

QUESTIONS

126) What famous writer was a cofounder of *The Village Voice*?

127) Who was the long-term lover of Aristotle Onassis before he married Jackie Kennedy?

128) What famous woman has been portrayed on the silver screen by Theda Bara, Claudette Colbert, Vivien Leigh, and Elizabeth Taylor?

129) What British general ordered the execution of Nathan Hale?

130) Who was the social-register aristocrat who became one of Andy Warhol's "underground" stars before dying a tragic death?

131) What British female pop singing star of the 1960s and early 1970s was a child actress in the 1940s and '50s?

132) Which of the following was *not* invented by Thomas A. Edison?
   a. phonograph
   b. microphone
   c. photoelectric cell
   d. stock ticker

133) Who was the only American soldier to be executed for desertion since the Civil War?

134) Tennessee Williams was born and raised in Tennessee. True or false?

135) Who was the self-proclaimed "law west of the Pecos"?

. . . Answers

126. Norman Mailer

127. Maria Callas

128. Cleopatra

129. General Howe

130. Edie Sedgwick

131. Petula Clark

132. c

133. Eddie Slovik

134. False

135. Judge Roy Bean

136) What is the real name of "The Captain" of the musical couple The Captain & Tennille?

137) Dustin Hoffman grew up in:
    a. Cleveland
    b. Toronto
    c. New York City
    d. Los Angeles

138) Who is the newly elected President of El Salvador?

139) What American sergeant lost both of his hands in combat during World War II and then went on to act in a single movie for which he won two Oscars?

140) Who was Jack Benny's wife?

141) Former CIA agent Edwin P. Wilson was put in prison for delivering armaments illegally to what foreign nation?

142) What actor/comedian learned to play the saxophone and speak Russian for a role in a movie?

143) Here are the first names of a father and two daughters of a well-known theatrical family: Richard, Joan, and Constance. What is their last name?

144) What star of 1930s Hollywood westerns left show business to become the lieutenant governor of Nevada?

145) One-time head of the Environmental Protection Agency, Anne Gorsuch was married while in office. What was her name when she resigned?

. . . *Answers*

136. Daryl Dragon

137. d

138. Jose Napoleon Duarte

139. Harold Russell (for *The Best Years of Our Lives*)

140. Mary Livingstone

141. Libya

142. Robin Williams (*Moscow on the Hudson*)

143. Bennett

144. Rex Bell

145. Anne Buford

146) James Clavell, author of *Shogun*, also produced and directed what motion picture starring Sidney Poitier?

147) Harold Washington is the first black mayor of what major U.S. city?

148) Who was the founder of the influential French film magazine *Cahiers du Cinema*?
   a. Andre Bazin
   b. Francois Truffaut
   c. Louis Malle
   d. Jean-Luc Goddard

149) When asked why he left his home town of St. Louis, who replied, "Doesn't everybody?"

150) Wheeler and Woolsey were:
   a. a dance team
   b. a juggling act
   c. the hosts of a 1950s T.V. show
   d. a comedy team

151) Name any two of "The Hollywood Ten."

152) Radio comedian Fred Allen never appeared in a movie. True or false?

153) The first names John, Lionel, and Ethel belong to what famous theatrical family?

154) The Pied Piper of Hameln was a real person. True or false?

. . . Answers

146. *To Sir With Love*

147. Chicago

148. a

149. Vincent Price

150. d

151. Alvah Bessie, Herbert Biberman, Lester Cole, Edward Dmytryk, Ring Lardner Jr., John Howard Lawson, Albert Maltz, Sam Ornitz, Adrian Scott, and Dalton Trumbo.

152. False (He appeared in several movies.)

153. The Barrymore family

154. True

155) What still-living Gestapo officer was known as "The Butcher of Lyons"?

156) The play and movie versions of *The Barretts of Wimpole Street* is about the love affair of what two real-life people?

157) Name Hollywood's only woman director of the 1930s.

158) Desiderio Alberto Arnaz y de Acha is the full name of what well-known TV personality?

159) Who gave Charo's entertainment career a big boost?

160) What outlaw labor-union leader recently won the Nobel Peace Prize?

161) What are the first names of the famous husband-and-wife acting team of Lunt and Fontanne?

162) Who is the *real* mother of Dallas's "J.R."?

163) What is the name of the dancer who actually did the fancy footwork in the hit movie *Flashdance*?

164) Dianne, Janet, Kathy, and Peggy are a sister singing group. What is their last name?

165) Australian actor Mel Gibson (*The Year of Living Dangerously*) was born in:
    a. Peekskill, N.Y.
    b. Brooklyn, N.Y.
    c. Sydney, Australia
    d. Darling Downs of Queensland, Australia

. . . *Answers*

155. Klaus Barbie

156. Robert Browning and Elizabeth Barrett (Browning)

157. Dorothy Arzner

158. Desi Arnaz

159. Xavier Cugat

160. Lech Walesa

161. Alfred Lunt and Lynn Fontanne

162. Actress Mary Martin

163. Marine Jahan

164. Lennon (The Lennon Sisters)

165. a

166) Who is the president pro tempore of the U.S. Senate?

167) What famous French film director is married to American actress Candice Bergen?

168) Elizabeth Taylor once called this film star the most beautiful woman in the world. Who was Liz referring to?

169) Legendary stage actress Sarah Bernhardt never acted in a movie. True or false?

170) John Roebling designed what famous bridge?

171) What was Perry Como's occupation before he was a singing star?

172) Which of the Gabor sisters, Eva or Zsa Zsa, is the younger?

173) One-time music star Cat Stevens is now a penniless beggar in what foreign country?

174) Whom has Fred Astaire named as his favorite dance partner?

175) Frank Sinatra's wife Barbara was once married to what famous comedian?

176) Which of the following was once a former top-level auto executive?
    a. Wallace Ford
    b. Paul Ford
    c. Jeffrey Packard
    d. George Romney

. . . Answers

166. Senator Strom Thurmond (R-S.C.)

167. Louis Malle

168. Ava Gardner

169. False (She made several silent films.)

170. The Brooklyn Bridge

171. Barber

172. Eva

173. Iran

174. Gene Kelly

175. Zeppo Marx

176. d

177) What dress designer claims she was denied the opportunity to buy a New York City apartment because of her involvement with a black musician?

178) Who were the two wiz kids in their twenties who started Apple Computers?

179) Irving Berlin began his musical career as a singing waiter. True or false?

180) Who was Ray Stark's first choice for the title role in the Broadway production of *Funny Girl*?
   a. Anne Bancroft
   b. Barbra Streisand
   c. Shirley Maclaine
   d. Shirley Jones

181) What noted film director of horror and suspense was allowed as a child to watch his surgeon father perform operations?

182) *Harper's Bazaar* did *not* choose which of the following in their list of the top ten most beautiful actresses of 1983?
   a. Twiggy
   b. Joan Collins
   c. Victoria Principal
   d. Meryl Streep

183) Noah Beery Jr., who played James Garner's father in *The Rockford Files,* is the nephew of what famous actor?

184) What do former "First Brother" Billy Carter and August A. Busch have in common?

. . . Answers

177. Gloria Vanderbilt (The black musician was Bobby Short.)

178. Stephen Wozniak and Steven Jobs

179. True

180. a

181. Brian de Palma

182. d

183. Wallace Beery

184. Both had beer brands named after them ("Billy Beer" and "Busch.")

QUESTIONS

185) What multitalented Academy-award-winning director failed a college course in motion-picture production?

186) Paul Anka's hit song "Puppy Love" was about his relationship with what young actress?

187) What was President Gerald R. Ford's original name?

188) Who is the father of Vanessa Redgrave's illegitimate child?

189) Warren Beatty is the famous actor/director's real name. True or false?

190) Which U.S. president used to escort his future wife to meet her other boyfriends?

191) F. Scott Fitzgerald had a grand romance at the end of his life that wasn't with Zelda. Who was the lady?

192) Who was the first black American to have a novel published in the U.S.?

193) Who invented the process to make condensed milk?

194) Richard Basehart was a politician before he became an actor. True or false?

195) Dr. Paul Ehrlich developed a treatment for:
    a. gonorrhea
    b. smallpox
    c. diptheria
    d. syphilis

. . . *Answers*

185. Woody Allen

186. Annette Funicello

187. Leslie Lynch King, Jr. (He was adopted.)

188. Franco Nero

189. False (It's Warren Beatty.)

190. Richard Nixon

191. Sheilah Graham

192. William Wells Brown (*Clotelle: or The President's Daughter*, 1853.)

193. Gail Borden

194. True

195. d

196) Which of the following did *not* receive a 1983 "Outstanding Mother Award" from the National Mother's Day Committee?

    a. Senator Paula Hawkins
    b. Barbara Mandrell
    c. Erma Bombeck
    d. Ellen Burstyn

197) President Dwight D. Eisenhower was a voracious reader of westerns by what author?

198) Football coach Frank Kush coached what future baseball star at Arizona State University?

199) What is the name of David Letterman's dog?

200) Henry Kissinger's wife Nancy played on her women's basketball team in college. True or false?

201) Who was the first black woman to star in the Folies Bergères?

202) What do Caroll Baker, Tammy Grimes, Debbie Reynolds, and Judy Garland all have in common?

203) What actress, who starred in the 1960 hit movie *Where The Boys Are*, gave up her film career to become a nun?

204) Who was the only woman ever to own a movie studio?

205) What two New York Yankee pitchers swapped wives and families?

. . . Answers

196. c

197. Louis L'amour

198. Reggie Jackson

199. Bob

200. False

201. Josephine Baker

202. They all have daughters with successful show-business careers.

203. Dolores Hart

204. Alice Guy Blaché (1915, Sun Pictures, Fort Lee, N.J.)

205. Mike Kekich and Fritz Peterson

206) What famous member of a comedy team smuggled secret papers out of Russia?

207) Who was the first man in space?

208) What is Michael Jackson's father's name?

209) What is Mr. T's favorite TV show?

210) In 1848, when he died, he was the richest man in America. Who was he?

211) Hugh Hefner was once engaged to Gloria Steinem. True or false?

212) Which of the following TV newsmen was a Rhodes scholar?
    a. Roger Mudd
    b. Tom Brokaw
    c. Howard K. Smith
    d. none of the above

213) When Stanley found Livingstone in Africa he said, "Dr. Livingstone, I presume?" What were Stanley's and Livingstone's first names?

214) What was the manner of death of Balboa, the famous Spanish conquistador who discovered the Pacific Ocean?
    a. drowning
    b. beheaded
    c. old age
    d. scurvy

. . . *Answers*

206. Harpo Marx (He did it upon the request of the U.S. Ambassador.)

207. (Russian cosmonaut) Yuri Gagarin

208. Joe Jackson

209. *The Beverly Hillbillies*

210. John Jacob Astor

211. False

212. c

213. Henry (Stanley) and David (Livingstone)

214. b

215) Actress Ingrid Bergman is related to director Ingmar Bergman. True or false?

216) What was the last name of the English land agent in Ireland whose ruthlessness led his employees to refuse to cooperate with him?

217) Bette Davis and Henry Fonda once dated each other as teenagers. True or false?

218) What musical instruments does each of the following play?
   a. George Segal
   b. Dudley Moore
   c. Woody Allen
   d. Johnny Carson

219) When Sir Francis Drake sailed around the world in the sixteenth century, it took him:
   a. one year
   b. two years
   c. three years
   d. four years

220) What three-time presidential candidate took on lawyer Clarence Darrow in the famous Scopes Monkey Trial?

221) The famous lover, Casanova, was from what Italian city?

222) Who was the test pilot that broke the sound barrier in 1947?

. . . *Answers*

215. False

216. Boycott

217. True

218. a. Segal-banjo b. Moore-piano c. Allen-clarinet d. Carson-drums

219. c

220. William Jennings Bryan

221. Venice

222. Chuck Yeager

223) What comedienne, who became famous on TV, made her Broadway debut in *New Faces of 1934* performing a mock striptease?

    a. Lucille Ball
    b. Imogene Coca
    c. Vivian Vance
    d. Eve Arden

224) What did actor Jimmy Stewart do during World War II?

225) Actor Tyrone Power was once married to a French actress with just one name, which was:

    a. Annabella
    b. Babette
    c. Colette
    d. Damita

226) What recent Oscar nominee is an actor, playwright, rock musician, poet, and rodeo rider?

227) What was the name of Mahatma Gandhi's assassin?

228) "Get that bastard off the lot, *now*! I never want to see him again until we need him." Who said it?

229) In 1960, what husband-and-wife team performed in a G.E. Theater TV production of *A Turkey For The President*?

230) Cyrano de Bergerac was a real person, not just a fictional character. True or false?

231) What member of one of the most important rock bands of the late 1960s quit his group in 1971 to become a poet — and died that same year at the age of 27?

. . . *Answers*

223. b

224. He was a bomber pilot in Europe.

225. a

226. Sam Shepard

227. Nathuran Godse

228. Samuel Goldwyn

229. Ronald Reagan and Nancy Davis (Reagan)

230. True

231. Jim Morrison

232) What English general was defeated by George Washington at Yorktown?

233) Newspaperman Horace Greeley ran for president in 1872. True or false?

234) In what year was actress Joan Collins born?
   a. 1933
   b. 1936
   c. 1939
   d. 1940

235) Alexander Fleming was the bacteriologist who, in 1928, discovered what important new drug?

236) What King of Babylonia established the first written code of laws?

237) What famous British actor with a mellifluous voice became a Hollywood star despite his wooden leg?

238) Actress Gina Lollobrigida has established herself in what other artistic career?

239) What New York City mayor was known as the "Little Flower"?

240) The clever guerrilla leader of the American Revolution, Francis Marion, was known by what nickname?

241) What former Republican Senate minority leader cut a hit record in the 1960s?

242) What was Paul Revere's occupation?

. . . Answers

232. Cornwallis

233. True

234. a

235. Penicillin

236. Hammurabi

237. Herbert Marshall

238. Photography

239. Fiorello LaGuardia

240. "The Swamp Fox"

241. Everett M. Dirksen

242. Silversmith

43) Who was the Mexican general who attacked the Alamo?

44) John D. Rockefeller made the family fortune in oil. He spent some of that money by endowing what midwestern university?

45) Who was the hairdresser who served as the inspiration for Warren Beatty's character in the movie *Shampoo*?

46) "Old Blood and Guts" was the nickname of what American World War II general?

47) Hans Christian Andersen of fairy tale fame was:
   a. Swedish
   b. Danish
   c. Norwegian
   d. German

48) Which of the following had a well-publicized affair with Marilyn Monroe?
   a. Yves Montand
   b. Jean-Paul Belmondo
   c. Jacques Brel
   d. Charles Aznavour

49) Akio Morita is the Japanese physicist and business executive who founded what major company?

50) What is the name of Barbra Streisand's younger half-sister who is herself a singer?

51) Belle Starr, the famous female outlaw of the Old West, was married and had a child. True or false?

. . . Answers

243. Santa Anna

244. University of Chicago

245. Gene Shacov

246. George S. Patton, Jr.

247. b

248. a

249. Sony

250. Roslyn Kind

251. True

252) What teenager living in Milwaukee grew up to become an Israeli prime minister?

253) What is Sandra Dee's real name?

254) Frank Sinatra, Jr. was once a kidnapping victim. True or false?

255) James Agee was primarily known as a critic and novelist, but he also wrote the screenplay for what movie starring Humphrey Bogart?

256) Lowell Thomas was:
   a. a journalist
   b. an author
   c. a founder of Cinerama
   d. all of the above
   e. none of the above

257) Sigmund Freud's wife's name was Anna. True or false?

258) What star place-kicker for the New York Giants later became a well-known TV sportscaster?

259) What is rock 'n roll star Fabian's full name?

260) Name two former major-league sports stars who are now members of the U.S. Congress.

261) Johnny Carson once said, "She doesn't need a steak knife. _____ cuts her food with her tongue."

262) What "*marvelous*" major-league baseball player is now a spokesman for a beer company?

. . . Answers

252. Golda Meir

253. Alexandra Zuck

254. True

255. *The African Queen*

256. d

257. False (His wife was Martha; his daughter was Anna)

258. Pat Summerall

259. Fabian Forte Bonaparte

260. Senator Bill Bradley (N.Y. Knickerbockers) and Representative Jack Kemp (Buffalo Bills)

261. Rona (Barrett)

262. "Marvelous" Marv Throneberry

263) Eldridge Cleaver wrote *Soul On Ice* when he was:
   a. in Libya
   b. an expatriate in Paris
   c. in prison
   d. on the run from the Mafia

264) Who had a well-publicized affair with millionaire Alfred Bloomingdale?

265) Harry Anderson, star of TV's *Night Court*, has another show biz sideline. What is it?

266) Sidney Leibowitz is the real name of what well-known singer?

267) Which of the following actresses is from Sweden:
   a. Elke Sommer
   b. Liv Ullman
   c. Ann-Margret
   d. Ursula Andress

268) She's the daughter of a famous American director and the long-time girlfriend of Jack Nicholson. Who is she?

269) What famous star quarterback has appeared as an actor on Broadway?

270) Sammy Davis, Jr. appeared on a soap opera. True or false?

271) Actress/author Ruth Gordon is married to what well-known writer?

. . . *Answers*

263. c

264. Vicki Morgan

265. He's a magician.

266. Steve Lawrence

267. c

268. Anjelica Huston

269. Joe Namath

270. True (*One Life To Live*)

271. Garson Kanin

272) What actor dressed up as Santa Claus and had a once-a-year affair with actress Shelley Winters every Christmas for many years?

273) What glamorous comedy star reportedly took low colonoics every day in order to keep looking young?

274) Who was the founder of the National Broadcasting Company (NBC)?

275) Who was the only movie actor to play a monster without using any makeup?

276) T.V. journalist Geraldo Rivera was originally trained as a lawyer. True or false?

277) What is the nickname of the famous flyer who mistakenly flew to Ireland instead of to Los Angeles?

278) What writer is famous for physically putting himself into the center of his subject matter?

279) TV's Mr. Rogers is a Presbyterian minister. True or false?

280) What gangster of the 1920s was known as "Scarface"?

281) What is John DeLorean's wife's professional name?

282) Writer/director Luis Buñuel is:
    a. Italian
    b. Spanish
    c. French
    d. Brazilian

. . . *Answers*

272. William Holden

273. Mae West

274. David Sarnoff

275. Rondo Hatton

276. True

277. "Wrong Way" (Corrigan)

278. George Plimpton

279. True

280. Al Capone

281. Cristina Ferrare

282. b

283) What is Beverly Sills's nickname?

284) What famous actress once saved Montgomery Clift from choking to death?

285) "I've made over a million dollars in my life by not listening to men in blue suits." Who said it?

286) Joanne Woodward is Paul Newman's first wife. True or false?

287) Name the three famous actresses who have been married to actor John Derek.

288) What was the first name of Spencer Tracy's wife?

289) *Playboy* playmate and budding actress Dorothy Stratton was murdered by her husband. What was his name?

290) What eccentric, popular concert pianist made a successful side career in the movies (usually playing comedy) and even had his own syndicated TV talk show in the 1950s?

291) What is the name of physical fitness expert Jack La-Lanne's wife who has appeared with him on his TV show?

292) Who were the two participants in the so-called "Kitchen Debate"?

293) What famous King of Scotland was a leper?

294) Nu U was briefly President of South Vietnam in 1957. True or false?

. . . Answers

283. "Bubbles"

284. Elizabeth Taylor

285. Woody Allen

286. False

287. Ursula Andress, Linda Evans, and Bo Derek

288. Louise

289. Paul Snider

290. Oscar Levant

291. Elaine LaLanne

292. Nikita Khrushchev and Richard Nixon

293. Robert Bruce

294. False

295) Who said "Trust in God and keep your powder dry"?

296) Was "Voltaire" a real name or a pen name?

297) What English queen had seventeen children?

298) The movie and the short-lived TV series *Bob & Carol & Ted & Alice* was based on the real-life affairs of Robert Goulet and his (then) wife Carol Lawrence. True or false?

299) What famous soldier was born in Europe, died in Asia, and was laid to rest in Africa?

300) Billie Burke who played Glinda, the Good Witch in *The Wizard of Oz*, was the widow of what famous man?
   a. Robert Benchley
   b. Leslie Howard
   c. George M. Cohan
   d. Florenz Ziegfeld

301) "Wild Bill" Hickock was killed in a poker game. What was his "Dead Man's Hand"?

302) What well-known singer once blocked Johnny Carson's attempt at buying the Aladdin Hotel in Las Vegas?

303) Gonzo journalist Hunter Thompson has been portrayed on the silver screen by what actor/comedian?

304) What movie star commissioned the building of a nude statue of his actress wife for his lawn?

. . . *Answers*

295. Oliver Cromwell

296. A pen name (His real name was Francoise Marie Arouet.)

297. Queen Anne

298. False (The story was purely fictional.)

299. Alexander the Great

300. d

301. "Aces and Eights"

302. Wayne Newton

303. Bill Murray (in *Where The Buffalo Roam*)

304. Tyrone Power

305) Winston Churchill's mother, Jennie, was:
   a. English
   b. Irish
   c. Canadian
   d. American

306) What was the name of newsman Chet Huntley's Montana resort?

307) What famous Welsh actor is a hemophiliac?

308) Which of the following famous people does *not* paint as a hobby?
   a. Harry Reasoner
   b. Norman Mailer
   c. Jimmy Cagney
   d. Red Skelton

309) What title does comedian Henny Youngman claim?

310) Robert Redford suffers from:
   a. vertigo
   b. claustrophobia
   c. agoraphobia
   d. none of the above

311) Alfred B. Nobel, who established the Nobel Peace Prize, was also a famous inventor. What is his best known invention?

312) Who was the lawyer who prosecuted Charles Manson in the famous Sharon Tate murder case?

. . . *Answers*

305. d

306. "Big Sky"

307. Richard Burton

308. b

309. "King of the One-Liners"

310. b

311. Dynamite

312. Vincent Bugliosi

313) What actress created the role of Dorothy in the stage version of *The Wiz* and then returned to play the same role on Broadway nine years later?

314) Baseball Commissioner Bowie Kuhn is a descendant of what famous hero of the Old West?

315) Which of the following celebrities was *not* born in Philadelphia?
  a. Frankie Avalon
  b. Bill Cosby
  c. Jacqueline Susann
  d. Ruth Buzzi

316) What former U.S. Ambassador to Britain is also a famous publisher?

317) What was the name of the Lindberghs' baby?

318) How tall is Danny De Vito (Louie De Palma) of *Taxi*?

319) What member of a famous comedy duo was a former stuntman?

320) Fred Astaire was born in:
  a. New York City
  b. London
  c. Omaha
  d. St. Louis

321) What Hollywood studio head arm-wrestled both Jack Dempsey and Gene Tunney — *and won*?

. . . *Answers*

313. Stephanie Mills

314. Jim Bowie

315. d

316. Walter H. Annenberg (*T.V. Guide*)

317. Charles Lindbergh, Jr.

318. 5'0"

319. Lou Costello

320. c

321. Darryl F. Zanuck

QUESTIONS

322) CBS–TV once agreed to build a television studio in Florida next to what star's favorite golf course?

323) What entertainer used a ukelele as his trademark?

324) What actress's intimately detailed diary went public in her 1930s divorce trial and caused a scandal?

325) Who was Ronald Reagan's first wife?

326) Mel Ferrer was the first husband of what famous actress?

327) Who was the victim of the first political kidnapping in American history?

328) New York Yankee owner George Steinbrenner's money comes from what enterprise other than baseball?

329) Who did Oscar Wilde's fiancée marry?

330) What was the name of the 1971 Miss America who became the first female sportscaster on the staff of a TV network?

331) Who was the brilliant tactician who plotted military strategy for the North Vietnamese army against both the French and the Americans?

332) What real-life popular dancing couple was portrayed by Fred Astaire and Ginger Rogers in a 1939 film?

333) What are the first names of Rowan and Martin, the stars of TV's *Laugh-In*?

. . . *Answers*

322. Jackie Gleason

323. Arthur Godfrey

324. Mary Astor

325. Jane Wyman

326. Audrey Hepburn

327. Patty Hearst

328. Shipbuilding

329. Bram Stoker (author of *Dracula*)

330. Phyllis George

331. General Giap

332. Irene and Vernon Castle

333. Dan (Rowan) and Dick (Martin)

334) What singing group did Judy Garland belong to before she became a star?

335) Timothy Bottoms has two other actor brothers. What are their names?

336) Actors Jeff Bridges and Beau Bridges have a famous father. What is his name?

337) The first recipient of an artificial heart was Barney Clark. What was his profession?

338) Actor Warner Baxter was the father of actress Anne Baxter. True or false?

339) Alice Faye and Cyd Charisse were both married to what popular singer of his day?

340) What is the name of the famous female vocalist who's sorry now her father put her in a mental institution?

341) From what country did tennis champion Martina Navratilova defect?

342) Who is the famous baseball announcer known for saying, "Going, going . . . gone!" whenever a home run was hit?

343) What T.V. journalist is known as "The Eight Million Dollar Man"?

344) Who is the youngest of the Beatles?

345) What is George Burns's real name?

. . . *Answers*

334. The Gumm Sisters

335. Joseph and Sam

336. Lloyd Bridges

337. Dentist

338. False

339. Tony Martin

340. Connie Francis

341. Czechoslovakia

342. Mel Allen

343. Dan Rather

344. George Harrison (One year younger than Paul)

345. Nathan Birnbaum

QUESTIONS

346) Which of the following well-known personalities has *not* run for the office of mayor of New York City:
   a. Gore Vidal
   b. William F. Buckley
   c. Norman Mailer

347) Famous astronomer Copernicus was:
   a. German
   b. Polish
   c. Hungarian
   d. Dutch

348) What famous entertainer used the closing line, "Good night Mrs. Calabash, wherever you are"?

349) What movie actress, who starred in *The Summer of 42*, accidentally shot herself in the stomach?

350) Desilu Studios was created by what husband-and-wife team?

351) Who is known as "the world's oldest teenager"?

352) Chevy Chase's real name is:
   a. Charles Chase
   b. Charles Chatworth
   c. Chevalier Chase Beaudine
   d. Chevy Chase

353) Who was the first black performer to have his own network TV show?

354) What famous singing cowboy owns the California Angels baseball team?

. . . *Answers*

346. a

347. b

348. Jimmy Durante

349. Jennifer O'Neill

350. Desi Arnaz and Lucille Ball

351. Dick Clark

352. d

353. Nat King Cole (1957)

354. Gene Autry

355) What author and his novel were put on trial in France in 1857 for "lasciviousness and immorality," causing the book to become an instant best seller?

356) Name the three Andrew Sisters.

357) Commodore (Cornelius) Vanderbilt made his fortune in which two of these endeavors?
   a. the railroad
   b. steamship company
   c. Erie Canal
   d. fur trade

358) What Southern California town is named after a character made famous by Edgar Rice Burroughs?

359) Singer/songwriter/actor Kris Kristofferson was once a teacher at what famous institution?

360) What noted scholar posthumously became a media star when his TV show, *The Ascent of Man*, was aired on PBS?

361) Claudine Longet, ex-wife of singer Andy Williams, shot and killed what famous American skier?

362) Jack Benny helped make "Rochester" famous. What was Rochester's real name?

363) The famous Nelson family of TV's *Ozzie and Harriet* spawned rock 'n roll star Rickey Nelson. What is the name of the other Nelson son?

364) What is the name of the Russian Czar's daughter who might — or might not — have survived the Russian revolution?

. . . Answers

355. Gustave Flaubert's *Madame Bovary*

356. Patty, Maxine, and Laverne

357. a & b

358. Tarzana, CA (for the character, Tarzan)

359. West Point

360. Dr. Jacob Bronowski

361. Spider Sabitch

362. Eddie Anderson

363. David Nelson

364. Anastasia

365) The famous Mercury Theater was founded by what renowned actor/director?

366) What well-known actor is the father of star Alan Alda?

367) Where did western heroes Jim Bowie and Davy Crockett die?

368) What real-life woman of the Old West has been portrayed in the movies by Jean Arthur, Jane Russell, Yvonne de Carlo, Doris Day, and many others?

369) All of the following won the first "Best-Looking Hair Award" of 1983: Tom Selleck, Sylvester Stallone, Patrick Duffy, George Hamilton, and Rick Springfield. True or false?

370) Larry played the harmonica and composed music; Luther was in the movies; Stella made her name on Broadway. They were all siblings. What was their last name?

371) Name America's first woman astronaut.

372) Eddie Fisher was the best friend of one of Elizabeth Taylor's husbands. Name him.

373) To how many women has rock 'n roller Jerry Lee Lewis been married?

374) Actress and wealthy socialite Dina Merrill is married to what well-known actor?

375) How old was Stevie Wonder when he signed with Motown Records?

. . . Answers

365. Orson Welles

366. Robert Alda

367. The Alamo

368. Calamity Jane

369. True

370. Adler

371. Sally K. Ride

372. Mike Todd

373. Six

374. Cliff Robertson

375. Ten years old

376) Adlai E. Stevenson was all of the following *except*:
    a. Senator from Illinois
    b. Governor of Illinois
    c. U.N. Ambassador
    d. Presidential candidate

377) Who was the father of famed filmmaker Jean Renoir?

378) Rolling Stone Mick Jagger and model Jeri Hall had a baby girl. What's the infant's name?

379) What person who is associated with "Watergate" wrote a book about John Belushi?

380) What are the first names of the aviator Wright Brothers and the singing Wright Brothers?

381) Actress Carrie Fisher and recording artist Art Garfunkel are married. True or false?

382) In her youth this celebrity was the "Chief Coordinator" for the Eddie Fisher Fan Clubs. What is her name?

383) Who was on the cover of the first issue of *People Magazine*?

384) A major-league baseball player lost a leg but still continued his career as a pitcher. A film starring Jimmy Stewart was made of his heroic achievement. What was his name?

385) Who among the following is not associated with fire?
    a. Albert Camus   c. José Feliciano
    b. Michael Jackson   d. Richard Pryor

. . . *Answers*

376. a

377. Pierre Auguste Renoir (the celebrated French Impressionist painter)

378. Elizabeth Scarlett

379. Bob Woodward

380. Orville and Wilber (the aviators), Tom and Tim (the singers)

381. False (Carrie married Paul Simon.)

382. Rona Barrett

383. Mia Farrow

384. Monty Stratton

385. a

386) What was Humphrey Bogart's middle name?

387) George Wallace is the only four-term governor in Alabama history. True or false?

388) Where was Angela Lansbury (theater's "Mame") born?
    a. London
    b. Boston
    c. Brooklyn
    d. Las Vegas

389) Who is the youngest of Frank Sinatra's children?

390) Who shot Jesse James?

391) Writer Studs Terkel (*Working*) was a regular on a TV comedy show. True or false?

392) Who was the highly regarded programming executive at ABC–TV who made that network's prime-time schedule #1 in the late 1970s?

393) What 18th-century writer was known as "the inspired idiot"?

394) What is former quarterback, sportscaster, and actor Don Meredith's nickname?

395) In 1983 it was proven without doubt that famous aviatrix Amelia Earhart was shot down and killed over China by the Japanese. True or false?

396) What English queen had six fingers on one hand?

. . . Answers

386. DeForest

387. True

388. a

389. Tina Sinatra

390. Robert (Bob) Ford

391. True (*Stud's Place*, 1950)

392. Fred Silverman

393. Oliver Goldsmith

394. "Dandy" Don Meredith

395. False

396. Anne Boleyn

397) Pearl Buck, author of *The Good Earth*, was the wife of explorer Frank Buck. True or false?

398) What is the name of Lee Harvey Oswald's widow?

399) Name the U.S. Senate majority leader and the Speaker of the House.

400) Marlon Brando has an older sister who is an actress. True or false?

401) What was the name of the movie mogul whose daughter, Irene, married David O. Selznick?

402) Mel Blanc is the voice of Donald Duck. True or false?

403) Who is playwright David Rabe's Hollywood wife?

404) *The King and I* was based on the story of a real life Anna. True or false?

405) What is Bing Crosby's real first name?

406) Who was the English Archbishop of Canterbury martyred in 1170?

407) What famous TV talk-show host is an ex-altar boy from Cleveland?

408) Former pitching great Sandy Koufax married the daughter of what well-known actor?

409) What was the pen name of Oxford mathematician-turned-writer C.L. Dodgson?

. . . Answers

397. False

398. Marina Oswald (also known as Marguerite Oswald)

399. Senator Howard Baker (Majority Leader) and Rep. Tip O'Neil (Speaker)

400. True (Jocelyn Brando)

401. Louis B. Mayer

402. False (Clarence Nash)

403. Jill Clayburgh

404. True

405. Harry

406. Thomas à Becket

407. Phil Donahue

408. Richard Widmark (Anne Heath Widmark)

409. Lewis Carroll

QUESTIONS

410) Maria Shriver, one of the Kennedy cousins, has been the steady date of what imposing celebrity?

411) What was famous western writer Max Brand's real name?

412) What were the last names of gangsters Bonnie and Clyde?

413) Actor Leonard Nimoy wrote a very personal book. What was its title?

414) Who is the famous sister of actress Olivia De Havilland?

415) "Dere's a million good-looking guys in da world, but I'm a novelty." Who said it?

416) What real-life policeman served as the model for "Popeye" Doyle (Gene Hackman) in the movie *The French Connection*?

417) *Hellzapoppin* was a hit play and movie starring the comedy team of Olsen and Johnson. What famous comedian recently tried without success to revive the play?

418) What are the names of Ernest Hemingway's two actress granddaughters?

419) Actor Tony Perkins, noted for his performance in *Psycho*, has also sung on his own albums. True or false?

420) Who was England's answer to Marilyn Monroe?

421) Who was Yuri Andropov's successor?

. . . *Answers*

410. Arnold Schwarzeneggar

411. Frederick Faust

412. Bonnie Parker and Clyde Barrow

413. *I Am Not Spock*

414. Actress Joan Fontaine

415. Jimmy Durante

416. Eddie Egan

417. Jerry Lewis

418. Mariel & Marguax Hemingway

419. True

420. Diana Dors

421. Konstantin Chernenko

QUESTIONS

422) Who turned a Campbell's soup can into a piece of pop art in the 1960s?

423) Who is the syndicated Chicago columnist who served as the inspiration for the character portrayed by John Belushi in the movie *Continental Divide*?

424) How old was Barbra Streisand when she made her first trip out of Brooklyn? Where did she go?

425) John F. Kennedy, Jr. is a graduate of Harvard. True or false?

426) What is the full name of the man who invented the multicolored game cube that has 42.3 quintillion potential combinations?

427) Which of the following actors worked in New York's Yiddish Theater?
   a. Charles Ruggles
   b. Paul Muni
   c. Frederic March
   d. Elia Kazan

428) What was the name of Olympic decathalon winner Bruce Jenner's first wife?

429) What single-named hairdresser created Jackie Kennedy's bouffant hairdo?

430) Samuel Clemens was the first writer to use the pen name Mark Twain. True or false?

. . . *Answers*

422. Andy Warhol

423. Mike Royko

424. Fourteen years old. She went to Manhattan.

425. False (Brown University)

426. Ernö Rubik

427. b

428. Chrystie

429. Kenneth

430. False (It was originally used by Isaiah Sellers.)

431) Movie producer David Brown is married to what famous female of the magazine world?

432) Who was the lead singer of the 1960s group Herman's Hermits?

433) What ex-wife of a famous boxer was the oldest woman (age 54) to be used in a *Playboy* pictorial?

434) Which of the following stars has *not* been sued for palimony?
    a. Nick Nolte
    b. Rod Stewart
    c. Johnny Carson
    d. Flip Wilson

435) What do English physicians Richard Bright and Thomas Addison have in common?

436) Who is Pia Zadora's millionaire husband and mentor?

437) What was William Seward's "folly"?

438) Actor Erik Estrada (*CHIPS*) is:
    a. Mexican
    b. Puerto Rican
    c. Spanish
    d. Cuban

439) Noah Webster of dictionary fame and Daniel Webster, the politician, were cousins. True or false?

440) Who is the longest reigning English monarch in history?

. . . *Answers*

431. Helen Gurley Brown (*Cosmopolitan*)

432. Peter Noone

433. Vikki LaMotta

434. c

435. They both have diseases named after them.

436. Meshulum Ricklis

437. He bought Alaska.

438. b

439. False

440. Queen Victoria (64 years)

441) Andrew J. Volstead, an American legislator, was the author of the "Volstead Act," which prohibited what activity?

442) With which of the following singers has Michael Jackson *not* collaborated on a record?
   a. Paul McCartney
   b. Barbra Streisand
   c. Willie Nelson
   d. Johnny Mathis

443) Madame Marie Curie and her husband discovered radium. What was her husband's first name?

444) What do heart specialist Dr. Michael DeBakey and flier Charles A. Lindbergh have in common?

445) "Fatty" Arbuckle once performed in a Broadway play with Humphrey Bogart. True or false?

446) Who are the parents of Guy Davis, one of the stars in the recent movie *Beat Street*?

447) What female country western singing star has a home with fifteen bathrooms?

448) Brooke Shields's mother's name is Teri. What is Brookes's father's name?

449) Donald Sutherland was born in New Brunswick, New Jersey. True or false?

. . . *Answers*

441. Drinking alcohol

442. b, c, & d

443. Pierre

444. They both worked on developing an artificial heart.

445. True (*Baby Mine*, 1926)

446. Ossie Davis and Ruby Dee

447. Tammy Wynette

448. Frank Shields

449. False (New Brunswick, Canada)

450) Which of the following men did actress Paulette Goddard *not* marry?
- a. Burgess Meredith
- b. Charlie Chaplin
- c. Erich Maria Remarque
- d. Larry Parks

451) What was the name of Marilyn Monroe's drama coach?

452) What pen name did Agatha Christie use when she wrote a novel entitled *Haunted by Fear* in the 1930s?

453) Was Joan of Arc burned as a witch by the English or the French?

454) What singer of earthy songs caused a ruckus at a White House luncheon in 1968 over the Vietnam War?

455) Who is the actress Bette Davis once said she wished she looked like?

456) Former Vice President Hubert H. Humphrey's middle initial stood for:
- a. Hornblower
- b. Hilton
- c. Houston
- d. Horatio

457) U.S. Supreme Court Justice Oliver Wendell Holmes, Jr. became known by what descriptive phrase?

458) Who coined the expression, "Give the lady what she wants"?

. . . Answers

450. d

451. Natasha Lytess

452. Mary Westmacott

453. The English

454. Eartha Kitt

455. Katherine Hepburn

456. d

457. "The Great Dissenter"

458. Marshall Field

459) Francis Xavier Cabrini was the first U.S. citizen to be named a _____ by the Roman Catholic Church.

460) Neil Armstrong's Apollo moon-landing flight was his only trip in space. True or false?

461) "Cuddly" Dudley Moore has a very tall girlfriend. What is her name?

462) What is the last name of the U.S. naval commodore who opened ports of trade with Japan?

463) What was the name of the man Norma Jean Baker (Marilyn Monroe) married when she was sixteen years old?

464) Which of the following people is *not* associated with Andy Warhol?
    a. Paul Morrisey
    b. Holly Woodlawn
    c. Starbright Munk
    d. Joe Dellesandre

465) Roger Williams was the founder of Providence, Rhode Island, a place in which he hoped to provide religious freedom for:
    a. Huguenots
    b. Catholics
    c. Lutherans
    d. All faiths

466) Actress Jodie Foster is a student at what Ivy League university?

. . . *Answers*

459. Saint

460. False (Gemini 8 was his other flight in 1966.)

461. Susan Anton

462. Perry

463. Jim Dougherty

464. c

465. d

466. Yale

QUESTIONS

467) Oleg Cassini's brother Igor wrote a famous syndicated newspaper column in the 1950s and early 1960s under what name?

468) What was the name of the man who accused Alger Hiss of being a Communist spy?

469) Arnold Dorsey is the real name of what popular singer?

470) Who was known as "Mother of all the Russias"?

471) Alexandre Dumas wrote *The Thee Musketeers*. His son wrote *Camille*. What was his son's name?

472) Who was the first Chief Justice of the United States?

473) What sports champion has an "army" of spectators follow him whenever he plays?

474) The late *Playboy* centerfold and aspiring actress Dorothy Stratton was involved with what well-known movie director?

475) What famous singer was known for giving automobiles to complete strangers?

476) Jean-Paul Belmondo's son is the special friend of what celebrity?

477) Who was the first President of the Independent Republic of Texas?

478) What is Rona Barrett's married name?

. . . Answers

467. Cholly Knickerbocker

468. Whittaker Chambers

469. Engelbert Humperdinck

470. Catherine the Great

471. It was also Alexandre Dumas.

472. John Jay

473. Arnold Palmer ("Arnie's Army")

474. Peter Bogdanovich

475. Elvis Presley

476. Princess Stephanie of Monaco

477. Sam Houston

478. Mrs. William Allan Trowbridge

479) Dag Hammarskjold was the first U.N. Secretary-General. True or false?

480) With which of the following men has actress Farrah Fawcett not been romantically linked?
   a. James Caan
   b. Ryan O'Neal
   c. Lee Majors
   d. Burt Reynolds

481) Nurse Clara Barton was known as the "Angel of the Battlefield" during the American Civil War. She later founded what organization?

482) Was Johnny Appleseed a real person or a myth?

483) Actor Richard Dreyfus is related to the famous French soldier of the same last name who was sentenced to Devil's Island. True or false?

484) Name the two novelist Bronte sisters and state which wrote *Jane Eyre* and which wrote *Wuthering Heights*.

485) Helen Broderick, a comic relief character actress in the 1930s, is the mother of what famous actor?

486) Who was the founder of Boys' Town?

487) Whose trademark was white buckskin shoes?

488) What was the real name of "Billy the Kid"?

489) Tommy and Jimmy Dorsey, the popular bandleaders of the 1940s, were not related. True or false?

. . . *Answers*

479. False (Trygve Lie of Norway was first)

480. a

481. The American Red Cross

482. He was a real person (named John Chapman).

483. False

484. Charlotte — *Jane Eyre*; Emily — *Wuthering Heights*

485. Broderick Crawford

486. Father Flanagan

487. Pat Boone

488. William Bonney

489. False (They were brothers.)

490) In what high-risk business venture did Jimmy the Greek bet and lose?

491) What is the full name of the college football coach who was referred to as "Bear"?

492) What legendary soldier led the U.S. Marines against John Brown at Harper's Ferry in 1859?

493) "Looks like a Hawaiian bar mitzvah," was Blackwell's comment about what woman on his 1974 worst dressed list?
   a. Yoko Ono
   b. Dolly Parton
   c. Cher
   d. Bette Midler

494) The world's first test-tube baby, Louise Brown, was born in:
   a. South Africa
   b. The U.S.
   c. England
   d. Australia

495) Tom Parker, Elvis Presley's manager, is known by what title?

496) What about-to-become famous songwriter/singer was paid fifty dollars to play harmonica on a Harry Belafonte album in 1960?

497) Who was the first black American awarded the Nobel Peace Prize?

. . . *Answers*

490. Oil drilling (22 consecutive dry holes)

491. Paul Bryant (University of Alabama)

492. Robert E. Lee

493. c

494. c

495. Colonel

496. Bob Dylan

497. Ralph Bunche (in 1950)

QUESTIONS

498) What enigmatic U.S. vice president was once tried and acquitted for treason in a plot to set up his own independent empire in the West?

499) What singing star has had an assortment of pets that include a llama, deer, and a boa constrictor?

500) What member of the famous Kennedy clan married a marquis?

501) Who was the third person in the love triangle that led to Jean Harris's killing of Dr. Herman Tarnower?

502) How much were the Beatles paid for their first appearance on the *Ed Sullivan Show*?
- a. Nothing
- b. $2,400
- c. $12,000
- d. $16,800

503) Name the woman with whom Bob Guccione, publisher of *Penthouse Magazine*, has lived for more than nineteen years.

504) What is the ethnic background of Persis Khambatta, who was the female lead in *Star Trek — The Motion Picture*?

505) What is the name of Sonny Bono's third wife?

506) Marlon Brando once portrayed what Mexican revolutionary?

507) What actor/comedian made "noogies" famous?

. . . *Answers*

498. Aaron Burr

499. Michael Jackson

500. Kathleen ("Kick") Kennedy (The Marquis of Hartington)

501. Lynne Tryforos

502. b

503. Kathy Keeton

504. She's from India.

505. Susie Bono

506. Zapata

507. Bill Murray

508) What singer's hit song inspired the Dolly Parton/Sylvester Stallone movie *Rhinestone*?

509) The character played by Peter Falk in *Columbo* was based on a literary figure, Petrovich, who was a detective in a classic Russian novel by what author?

510) The expression, "In like flynn," was derived from the off-screen exploits of actor Errol Flynn. True or false?

511) What does Alan Hale, Jr. ("The Skipper" from *Gilligan's Island*) currently do for a living?

512) Who was the 1930s "platinum blonde" of Hollywood who lived hard and died young?

513) Charles Aznavour was the protegé of what famous singer?

514) Which of the following was a real frontier figure?
   a. Mike Fink
   b. Bronco Lane
   c. Brett Maverick
   d. Yancy Derringer

515) What wealthy and powerful man was behind the screen career of actress Marion Davies?

516) What is actor Jimmy Cagney's wife's nickname?

517) Sigourney Weaver, star of *Ghostbusters*, stands 5'10½" tall. True or false?

. . . Answers

508. Glen Campbell ("Rhinestone Cowboy")

509. Feodor Dostoevski (*Crime and Punishment*)

510. True

511. Owns and manages a seafood restaurant in L.A.

512. Jean Harlow

513. Edith Piaf

514. a

515. William Randolph Hearst

516. "Bill"

517. True

518) Barbara Jo Allen, who rose to fame on radio with Bob Hope, was also known as "Vera Vague." True or false?

519) How many times did Eugene Debs run for president?

520) What is the name of the woman who sued tennis star Billie Jean King for palimony?

521) Christina Crawford, who wrote *Mommie Dearest* about her mother, Joan, was adopted. True or false?

522) Author Nora Ephron (*Heartburn*) was married to what famous journalist?

523) Audie Murphy won more medals than any other solider in U.S. history. True or false?

524) Who was the Columbia Pictures head who forged actor Cliff Robertson's name on a $10,000 check?

525) Singer/songwriter Billy Joel has a famous model for a girlfriend. What is her name?

526) Alfred Hitchcock was once indicted for murder in the 1920s. True or false?

527) Shirley Temple was once married to actor John Agar. In 1948 they appeared together in a western movie. What was the name of the film?

528) In the 1957 movie *Fear Strikes Out* Tony Perkins played the role of what former Boston Red Sox player?

529) What star of *Taxi* is married to a star of *Cheers*?

. . . Answers

518. True

519. Five times (1900, 1904, 1908, 1912, and 1920)

520. Marilyn Barnett

521. True

522. Carl Bernstein (of Woodward and Bernstein fame)

523. False (Matt Urban, who belatedly received a total of 29 medals has more.)

524. David Begelman

525. Christie Brinkley

526. False

527. *Fort Apache*

528. Jimmy Piersall

529. Danny De Vito of *Taxi* is married to *Cheers'* Rhea Perlman.

530) What is Anne Bancroft's real name?

531) Dame Judith Anderson is English. True or false?

532) What famous TV personality and her cartoonist husband are the parents of twins?

533) Rock star Grace Jones's latest boyfriend is Swede Hans Lundgren, who is a champion of what sport?

534) What is the name of the female companion who lived with Groucho Marx during the last six years of his life?

535) What rock star, whose name is a combination of a "King" and a comic, once wrote this lyric: "I used to be disgusted/ Now I try to be amused"?

536) Tommy Sands was married to the daughter of what famous singer?

537) Carrie Snodgrass, who starred in the movie *Diary of a Mad Housewife*, left her burgeoning career to live with what rock star?

538) Silent screen comedian "Fatty" Arbuckle's career was destroyed in a 1921 sex scandal. Though he never acted again on screen, Arbuckle did direct occasionally. Under what name?

539) Who was the founder of *Time Magazine*?

540) "I had to be great. I couldn't be medium. My mouth was too big." Who said it?

. . . *Answers*

530. Anne Italiano

531. False (Australian)

532. Jane Pauley and Garry Trudeau

533. Kick-boxing

534. Erin Fleming

535. Elvis Costello

536. Frank Sinatra (Nancy was the daughter.)

537. Neil Young (They had a child, but split in 1975.)

538. "Will B. Good"

539. Henry Luce

540. Barbra Streisand

541) What actor (who always wears red socks) was in a serious car crash in the 1940s and survived with only a slight facial scar?

542) Who invented the Braille system of printing and writing for the blind?

543) Rodney Dangerfield was a close friend of comedian Lenny Bruce. True or false?

544) What was the maiden name of the woman who stuck with writer James Joyce till he died?

545) What former major-league left-handed baseball pitcher was known as "Space Man"?

546) What daughter of President Reagan used to live with a member of a rock 'n roll band?

547) Which members of the Beatles are left handed?

548) Marlon Brando had a son, Tehotu, with his Polynesian costar of *Mutiny on the Bounty*. What was her name?

549) In January, 1984, fashion designer Richard Blackwell announced his 23rd list of Worst-Dressed Women. Who was tied for tenth place with Houston Mayor Kathy Whitmire?

550) A famous author stabbed his wife and then wrote a novel about it. What is the author's name and what was the name of the book?

. . . *Answers*

541. Van Johnson

542. Louis C. Braille

543. True

544. Nora Barnacle

545. Bill Lee

546. Patti Davis (She lived with Eagles guitarist Bernie Leadon.)

547. Paul McCartney and Ringo Starr

548. Tarita

549. Dustin Hoffman (as "Dorothy" in his hit film, *Tootsie*)

550. Norman Mailer; *An American Dream*

551) What lead member of a Motown group started at Motown earning $35.00 per week as a secretary to Smokey Robinson?

552) "Johnny Carson" was the title of a song recorded by the Beach Boys. True or false?

553) When asked "Do you want to do the classics?" who replied, "I don't do Shakespeare. I don't talk in that kind of broken English"?

554) What was Fred Astaire's dancing partner/sister's name?

555) What American actress was the first to be called a "vamp"?

556) Who was the English actress known as the "Jersey Lily"?

557) Buster Crabbe and Johnny Weismuller both portrayed Tarzan, but only one of them was an Olympic champion. True or false?

558) Who was largely responsible for discovering and showcasing the Osmonds?

559) The woman "Julia" from the movie of the same name was a real-life friend of what writer?

560) Dr. Demento is:
    a. a psychiatrist/columnist
    b. an axe-murderer
    c. a disc jockey
    d. a rock 'n roll artist

. . . *Answers*

551. Martha Reeves (of Martha Reeves and the Vandellas)

552. True

553. Mr. T.

554. Adele

555. Theda Bara

556. Lily Langtry

557. False (Both were Olympic champions.)

558. Andy Williams

559. Lillian Hellman

560. c

QUESTIONS

561) What publishing company does Jackie Onassis work for?

562) What film star received a replacement Oscar at the 1983 Academy Awards ceremony because a fire destroyed the statue he had garnered in 1951?

563) Who was the mother of the man who would not be king, the Duke of Windsor?

564) Who created the influential *New York Magazine*?

565) He was a famous child actor. Later he became a TV executive, a director, and even played Clark Kent's boss Perry White. Who is he?

566) What is the name of the American girl who, at age eleven, visited Russia at the invitation of Yuri Andropov?

567) Joseph Kennedy, President John F. Kennedy's father, was America's ambassador to what country?

568) What is the name of John Belushi's widow?

569) Johnny Hyde was the agent who helped launch the career of what famous movie star?

570) Charles Lindbergh flew fifty combat missions against the Japanese in World War II as a civilian. True or false?

571) What well-known actress is the sister of writer/director Francis Ford Coppola?

. . . Answers

561. Doubleday

562. Gene Kelly

563. Queen Mary

564. Clay Felker

565. Jackie Cooper

566. Samantha Smith

567. Britain

568. Judy Jacklin

569. Marilyn Monroe

570. True

571. Talia Shire

572) What baseball star turned down a $100,000-a-year contract because he felt he hadn't earned it?

573) What teen idol of the late 1950s and early 1960s began his career as a trumpet player with a group called Rocco and the Saints?

574) Whom did Bob Woodward and Carl Bernstein of Watergate fame describe as the most "relentless interrogator" they ever faced?

575) Barbara Cartland, queen of the romance novels, is from:
    a. Michigan
    b. Maine
    c. France
    d. England

576) What famous actress is the granddaughter of architect Frank Lloyd Wright?

577) Bing Crosby's son Gary is a well-known young golfer. True or false?

578) In literary circles, writer Harry Stein is known as:
    a. Mr. Punctuation
    b. Mr. Complex Sentence
    c. Mr. Ethics
    d. Mr. Hoopla

579) What was the name of the famous family that allowed themselves to be filmed for a TV documentary that ultimately shattered their lives?

... *Answers*

572. Al Kaline (Detroit Tigers)

573. Frankie Avalon

574. Phil Donahue

575. d

576. Anne Baxter

577. False (Bing's son Nathanial Crosby is the golfer.)

578. c

579. The Loud Family

QUESTIONS

580) Which of the following was painted by Leonardo da Vinci?
   a. The Mona Lisa
   b. The First Supper
   c. Blue Boy
   d. Starry Night

581) What Panamanian-born baseball star observes Jewish holidays?

582) Hollywood's classy film director Ernest Lubitsch (famous for "The Lubitsch Touch") was once a silent screen movie comic in Germany. True or false?

583) What do Guy Madison and Betty Grable have in common?

584) What were the stage names of the two Marx Brothers who retired early?

585) John Hodiak was a movie star of the 1940s and the ex-radio voice of what well-known fictional country bumpkin?

586) What vaudeville comic (who later became a major TV star) gave Judy Garland her name?

587) Rock singer Stephen Stills auditioned to become a member of The Monkees. True or false?

588) Film critic Andrew Sarris is married to another eminent writer on film. What is her name?

589) Who is the former Olympic athlete and actor who worked as Bobby Kennedy's bodyguard?

. . . *Answers*

580. a

581. Rod Carew (His wife is Jewish.)

582. True

583. They were both the leading pin-ups during World War II. Guy Madison for women and Betty Grable for GIs.

584. Zeppo and Gummo

585. Li'l Abner

586. Milton Berle

587. True (He was rejected.)

588. Molly Haskell

589. Rafer Johnson

590) Who was the "Boop-boop-a-doop" girl?

591) Which of the following celebrities started his show-biz career as a disc jockey?
   a. Waylon Jennings
   b. B.B. King
   c. Soupy Sales
   d. All of the above
   e. None of the above

592) Ginger Rogers and Lola Lane were both married to what actor who portrayed a doctor created by writer Max Brand?

593) Lauren Bacall was Humphrey Bogart's:
   a. second wife
   b. third wife
   c. fourth wife
   d. fifth wife

594) Which of the following was a telegraph operator from Tioga, Texas and later became a famous singing cowboy?
   a. Roy Rogers
   b. Bronco Billy Anderson
   c. Gene Autry
   d. Monte Blue

595) Tom Dressen was part of a comedy team called Tim and Tom. Tim became a TV actor appearing as a regular on *Simon and Simon* and WKRP Cincinnati. What is Tim's last name?

596) What actress who played the title role *Annie* on Broadway survived a bout with cancer?

. . . *Answers*

590. Helen Kane

591. d

592. Lew Ayres (Dr. Kildare)

593. c

594. c

595. Reid

596. Shelly Bruce

QUESTIONS

597) Don Stroud (Captain Pat Chambers on TV's *Mickey Spillane's Mike Hammer*) got his start doubling for Troy Donahue on a surfboard. True or false?

598) Joan Crawford began her show business career as:
   a. a dancer
   b. a vaudeville magician's helper
   c. a ventriloquist
   d. a flutist

599) Who would have been Ronald Reagan's running mate had he gotten the Republican presidential nomination in 1976?

600) This Australian with a newspaper empire coproduced the hit movie *Gallipoli*. Who is he?

601) In "The Crime of the Century," Leopold and Loeb kidnapped and murdered what fourteen-year-old boy?

602) Celebrity Barbara Hutton, once married to Cary Grant, was the granddaughter and heir of what famous retailer?

603) Who reportedly bends spoons (and other kitchen utensils) with the power of his mind?

604) A would-be assassin with the unlikely nickname of "Squeaky" tried to kill what U.S. president?

605) The first American to die in the Revolutionary War was Guy Fawkes. True or false?

606) What designer was responsible for the women's topless bathing suit?

. . . Answers

597. True

598. a

599. Senator Richard Schweiker

600. Rupert Murdock

601. Bobby Franks

602. F.W. Woolworth

603. Uri Geller

604. Gerald R. Ford (Lynette "Squeaky" Fromme was a follower of Charles Manson.)

605. False (Crispus Attucks was the first.)

606. Rudi Gernreich

607) Who was the lawyer who defended Lee Harvey Oswald's killer, Jack Ruby?

608) Who invented trousers?

609) Muckraking columnist Jack Anderson is a practicing Mormon. True or false?

610) Who was famous for saying "I'm just an old country lawyer" during the Senate Watergate hearings?

611) Which of Marilyn Monroe's husbands bitterly complained, "If it hadn't been for her friends, she might still be alive"?

612) What is the name of Jacques Cousteau's research ship?

613) Father John Corridan was the real-life inspiration for the labor-reform priest in what famous movie?

614) What were the names of all four Warner brothers who formed the movie studio that still bears their family name?

615) Sue Carol was an actress who later became an agent and then married her "biggest" client. Who was he?

616) Who, other than her husband Robert Wagner, was on the boat the night when Natalie Wood drowned?

617) Kansas Senator Robert Dole's wife Elizabeth has what job in the Reagan administration?

618) Who was the first black woman to win the title of Miss America?

. . . *Answers*

607. Melvin Belli

608. "Beau" Brummel

609. True

610. Senator Sam Ervin

611. Joe Di Maggio

612. Calypso

613. *On The Waterfront*

614. Albert, Harry, Jack, and Sam

615. Alan Ladd

616. Christopher Walken

617. Secretary of Transportation

618. Vanessa Williams

619) How old was Mozart when he wrote his first symphony?

620) Chuck Conners (*The Rifleman*) played professional baseball for the Brooklyn Dodgers and the Chicago Cubs. True or false?

621) What famous male vocalist has the same name as the composer of the opera *Hansel and Gretel*?

622) Popular composer Cole Porter was actually a coal porter in a West Virginia coal mine as a youth. True or false?

623) Movie critic Roger Ebert won a Pulitzer Prize in 1975. True or false?

624) What actress claimed to have married Howard Hughes aboard a ship in 1949 and that the marriage was never legally dissolved?

625) What movie star, who once played Doc Holliday, was known in his early career as "The Hunk"?

626) Grandma Moses, otherwise known as painter Anna Marry Robertson Moses, lived to be how old?

627) What English poet and playwright is buried in Westminster Abbey in a sitting position?

628) The famous play and later movie *The Man Who Came To Dinner* was based on what real life person?

629) What were the real first names of Groucho, Chico, and Harpo?

. . . Answers

619. Nine years old

620. True

621. Engelbert Humperdinck

622. False

623. True

624. Terry Moore

625. Victor Mature

626. One hundred and one years old (1860-1961)

627. Ben Jonson

628. Alexander Woollcott

629. Julius (Groucho), Leonard (Chico), and Adolph (Harpo)

630) Orson Welles once performed the trick of sawing what famous actress in half?
    a. Ginger Rogers
    b. Marlene Dietrich
    c. Gloria Swanson
    d. Alice Faye

631) Where was actor Patrick McGoohan born?

632) James MacArthur (*Hawaii Five-O*) is the adopted son of Helen Hayes and Charles MacArthur. True or false?

633) Due to a legal decree he has chosen to mask himself in wraparound sunglasses, but Clayton Moore is still _____ .

634) What famous porno star claims she was forced at gunpoint to perform in her most famous film?

635) Laszlo Loewenstein was the Hungarian actor who rose to fame as:
    a. Peter Lorre   c. Ernie Kovacs
    b. Bela Lugosi   d. Danny Kaye

636) She was the beautiful comic actress who was married to Clark Gable. She died in a tragic plane crash in 1942. Who was she?

637) Which of the following rock 'n roll stars has a "star" on Hollywood Boulevard?
    a. Natalie Cole   d. All of the above
    b. Neil Sedaka   e. None of the above
    c. Peter Frampton

. . . Answers

630. b

631. America

632. True

633. The Lone Ranger

634. Linda Lovelace

635. a

636. Carole Lombard

637. d

638) Abraham Lincoln was murdered at Ford's Theater by John Wilkes Booth. What was the name of the play that night?

639) What famous non-Jewish actor made his theatrical debut crying out "Nothing will help" in Yiddish?

640) Legendary record producer Phil Spector wrote the song "To Know Him Is To Love Him," performed by The Teddy Bears. Where did he get the title?

641) Who was the ex-acrobat and professional baseball player who established a reputation for himself in 1930s as a big-mouthed comedian?

642) Olympic swimming champion Mark Spitz is presently engaged in what kind of business?

643) What was brilliant painter and sculptor Michelangelo's last name?
    a. Maillol
    b. Francesca
    c. Robbia
    d. Buonarroti

644) Who was the famous actress/singer wife of composer Kurt Weill? (Hint: she was immortalized in both the Louis Armstrong and Bobby Darin versions of the Weill hit "Mack the Knife.")

645) W.C. Fields once supposedly spiked what costarring child actor's orange juice with gin?

. . . Answers

638. *Our American Cousin*

639. Steve McQueen

640. From his father's gravestone

641. Joe E. Brown

642. Real estate

643. d

644. Lotte Lenya

645. Baby Le Roy

646) David John Moore Cornwall is the real name of what famous writer of spy novels?

647) Peter Lawford began his career as a child actor. True or false?

648) What was the real last name of "The Lane Sisters"?

649) Western writer Zane Grey once lived in Tahiti. True or false?

650) The founder and guiding light of Motown Records, Berry Gordy, Jr. is white. True or false?

651) What famous publisher bought a Boeing 747 for his own use and gave it the name "Capitalist Tool"?

652) Who invented the Moog Synthesizer?

653) The first "Dial-A-Joke" featured the humor of what famous comedian?

654) Mick Jagger had a child with his former wife, Bianca. What is the child's alliterative name?

655) Which of the following sports figures has *not* modeled men's underwear?
    a. Ken Norton
    b. Jim Palmer
    c. Reggie Jackson

656) She starred in the movie *Pinky* and was the first black star of Broadway. Who was she?

. . . *Answers*

646. John Le Carré

647. True

648. Mulligan

649. True

650. False (He's black.)

651. Malcolm Forbes (of *Forbes Magazine*)

652. Robert Moog

653. Henny Youngman

654. Jade Jagger

655. c

656. Ethel Waters

657) The "Mexican Spitfire" was Carmen Miranda. True or false?

658) What celebrity couple, when going through a divorce, divided their toilet tissue into two equal piles?

659) What powerful American gossip columnist was once herself a Broadway and silent-screen actress?

660) What is actor Stewart Granger's real name?

661) Which of the famous Gish sisters, Lillian or Dorothy, was the younger?

662) Elvis Presley was known as "The King" of rock 'n roll. Who was known in the movies as "The King"? (Hint: not King Kong)

663) Which of the following was *not* an ice-skating star?
    a. Sonja Henie   c. Dorothy Hamill
    b. Peggy Fleming   d. Suzy Chafee

664) Katherine Hepburn is a graduate of which of the following colleges?
    a. Vassar   c. Radcliffe
    b. Smith   d. Bryn Mawr

665) Which of the following men was *not* married to Rita Hayworth?
    a. Frank Sinatra   c. Orson Welles
    b. Dick Haymes   d. Prince Ali Khan

666) By what name was character actor George Hayes better known?

. . . Answers

657. False (Lupe Velez)

658. Dick Powell and Joan Blondell

659. Hedda Hopper

660. James Stewart

661. Dorothy

662. Clark Gable

663. d

664. d

665. a

666. "Gabby" Hayes

667) Who was "The Wizard of Menlo Park"?

668) How many wives did Henry VIII have?

669) What is the real name of disc jockey "Wolfman Jack"?
   a. Jack Wolfson
   b. Warren Jackson
   c. Robert Smith
   d. Jack Roberts

670) Who filmed for posterity the assassination of President John F. Kennedy?

671) What actor (when in character) rescued his family from birds, and (when a lifeguard in his youth) rescued twenty-two people from sharks in the Australian surf?

672) Who is the mother of all those Osmond children?

673) How old was Sue Lyon when she played Lolita in the movie?

674) Charles-Edouard Jeannerti-Gris is the real name of what famous modern architect who, among other projects, designed most of the new Indian city of Chandigarh in the 1950s?

675) Efrem Zimbalist, Jr. took violin lessons from Jascha Heifetz. True or false?

676) What real-estate tycoon owns the U.S.F.L. New Jersey Generals?

. . . *Answers*

667. Thomas Edison

668. Six

669. c

670. Abraham Zapruder

671. Rod Taylor (The movie was *The Birds*.)

672. Olive Osmond

673. Fourteen

674. Le Corbusier

675. True

676. Donald Trump

677) Bobby Fischer defeated what Soviet chess player in Iceland for the world championship in 1972?

678) Who was the Russian ambassador to Hungary during the 1956 uprising?

679) Dr. Charles Frederick Menninger discovered meningitis. True or false?

680) Whose singing voice was dubbed in for Natalie Wood in *West Side Story* and Audrey Hepburn in *My Fair Lady*?

681) *Ninotchka* was the 1939 movie with what unique advertising slogan that was used because of its star's past artistic reputation?

682) What was the name of Jimmy Carter's evangelist sister?

683) Alfred Newman was:
    a. a Pulitzer Prize-winning reporter
    b. a composer of film scores
    c. the name associated with *Mad Magazine*
    d. 14th Vice President of the United States

684) Was Rock Hudson ever married?

685) Jacqueline Bisset is a film producer. True or false?

686) What famous inventor, who was also an expert on teaching speech to the deaf, advised that a teacher be sought for Helen Keller?

. . . Answers

677. Boris Spassky

678. Yuri Andropov

679. False

680. Marni Nixon

681. "Garbo Laughs!"

682. Ruth Carter Stapleton

683. b (Sorry, *Mad Magazine* — Alfred *E.* Newman)

684. Yes (A two-year marriage to Phyllis Gates)

685. True (She produced as well as starred in the movie *Rich and Famous*.)

686. Alexander Graham Bell

687) Which of the following singers is the only one to have a number one hit?
   a. James Brown
   b. Steve Lawrence
   c. Bob Dylan
   d. Fats Domino

688) Alice B. Toklas was the long-time companion of what famous writer?

689) Who were the three men who served as vice president during Franklin D. Roosevelt's administrations?

690) Who is referred to as "the father of the atomic bomb"?

691) As the owner of the second largest chain of variety stores (Woolworth's was number one), he was exceptionally rich — but when his shoes would start to wear out, he'd still line them with paper. Who was he?

692) Whom did Lauren Becall marry after her husband Humphret Bogart died?

693) Who was Shelley Winters's acting coach?

694) Who reached the South Pole first?
   a. Robert Byrd
   b. Roald Amundsen
   c. Robert Falcon Scott
   d. None of the above

695) Who is the founder and "driving" force of "Mothers Against Drunk Drivers" (MADD)?

. . . Answers

687. b ("Go Away Little Girl")

688. Gertrude Stein

689. John Nance Garner, Henry Wallace, and Harry Truman

690. J. Robert Oppenheimer

691. S.S. Kresge

692. Jason Robards, Jr.

693. Charles Laughton

694. b

695. Candy Lightner

696) What Nazi leader killed himself in jail just before he was to be executed as a war criminal?

697) Who originated a famous amateur hour on radio in 1934?

698) Horace and John were two brothers who had a significant impact on the automobile business. What was their last name?

699) Which of the following is *not* a prominent entrepreneur?
   a. Marcel Bich
   b. Vincent Bendix
   c. George Bantam
   d. Clarence Birdseye

700) What is Twiggy's real name?

701) President Nixon's banker friend, Charles Rebozo, is known by what nickname?

702) "Baby Face" Nelson was a member of what famous criminal's gang?

703) The notorious Mary Mallon was known as _____?

704) What avowed segregationist governor of the 1960s had more blacks in his administration than any other governor in the nation?

705) What female actress committed suicide after an unhappy love affair with Rex Harrison?

. . . Answers

696. Herman Goering

697. Major Edward Bowes

698. Dodge

699. c

700. Lesley Hornby

701. "Bebe"

702. John Dillinger

703. "Typhoid Mary"

704. Lester Maddox (Governor of Georgia)

705. Carole Landis

706) Former Yippies Abbie Hoffman and Jerry Rubin once made an offer to buy the New York Yankees baseball team. True or false?

707) Mel Brooks, Woody Allen, Carl Reiner, and Neil Simon all belong to which of the following organizations:
    a. The Hillcrest Country Club Auxiliary
    b. Writers Against Sick Humor (WASH)
    c. a & b
    d. None of the above

708) Indira Gandhi is the daughter of what famous Indian?

709) The late Don Blocker (Hoss in *Bonanza*) grew up in New Jersey. True or false?

710) What was the name of John Lennon's first wife?

711) In the 1950s, Dr. Joyce Brothers came into prominence by winning which of the following?
    a. *The $64,000 Question*
    b. *The $64,000 Challenge*
    c. a & b
    d. None of the above

712) What country singer/songwriter (and sometimes actor) is known as "the country outlaw"?

713) Only one actor has played Bozo the Clown on TV. True or false?

714) He was a major-league baseball pitcher with the nickname "Bulldog," a sportscaster, and the author of a book that was the basis of a short-lived TV show. Who is he?

. . . *Answers*

706. False

707. d

708. Nehru

709. False (He grew up in West Texas.)

710. Cynthia

711. c

712. Willie Nelson

713. False (Dozens of people have played Bozo in local shows across the country.)

714. Jim Bouton, author of *Ball Four*

QUESTIONS

715) Actor Ed Asner was elected president of what labor union?

716) Alistair Cooke is a citizen of what nation?

717) What former TV talk-show host is also a pianist, composer, recording artist, and novelist?

718) What former national office holder is associated with the Latin phrase *Nolo Contendere*?

719) What tennis champion stopped playing professionally when he had a heart attack and quadruple bypass surgery in 1979?

720) Primrose Bordier received France's *Légion d'Honneur* for designing:
    a. The Eiffel Tower
    b. The Louvre
    c. The Excocet Missile
    d. Sheets

721) Actress Sissy Spacek began her career doing:
    a. Off-Off Broadway
    b. singing
    c. TV commercials
    d. modeling

722) Vivien Leigh became famous in *Gone With The Wind* playing a Southern belle. Where was she born?
    a. England
    b. Boston
    c. India
    d. New Zealand

. . . Answers

715. Screen Actor's Guild

716. The U.S.

717. Steve Allen

718. Vice President Spiro Agnew (who pleaded *Nolo Contendere* — no contest — to a charge of income tax evasion and resigned his office.)

719. Arthur Ashe

720. d

721. b

722. c

723) Who was the senior partner in the comedy team of Laurel and Hardy?

724) What actor (who had champagne thrown in his face in one movie and got shot by Barbara Stanwyck in another film) was a professional singer before becoming a movie star?

725) What does "T.S." in T.S. Eliot stand for?

726) Who performed the first successful human heart transplant?

727) Actor/composer/singer Anthony Newley was a child star. True or false?

728) Helen Keller was born deaf, dumb, and blind. True or false?

729) What member of the Algonquin Round Table said, "Wit has truth in it; wisecracking is simply calisthenics with words"?
- a. Robert Benchley
- b. Ruth Gordon
- c. Alexander Woollcott
- d. Dorothy Parker

730) What was former First Lady Pat Nixon's maiden name?

731) During the 13th century, what Asian leader ruled a kingdom that stretched from the Pacific Ocean to the Mediterranean Sea?

732) Who is the ventriloquist who gives voice to Knucklehead Smith?

. . . Answers

723. Stan Laurel

724. Fred MacMurray (champagne — *The Caine Mutiny;* shot — *Double Indemnity*)

725. Thomas Stearns

726. Dr. Christian Barnard

727. True

728. False (She was normal until the age of eighteen months when struck by scarlet fever.)

729. d

730. Ryan

731. Kublai Khan

732. Paul Winchell

733) Annie Glenn, wife of Senator John Glenn (the former astronaut), finally conquered a life-long problem. What was her problem?

734) What is the name of Patricia Neal's ex-husband who helped her recover from her stroke?

735) Former Governor Jerry Brown of California and singer Linda Rondstadt were secretly married on January 19, 1983. True or false?

736) Who was the founder and first president of the National Organization for Women (NOW)?

737) His name conjures up images of religion, but his two houses of rock 'n roll worship were The Fillmore East and The Fillmore West. What is his name?

738) Is "Halston" the famous designer's:
    a. first name
    b. middle name
    c. last name
    d. pseudonym

739) Comedienne Gilda Radner had a well-publicized affair with:
    a. Chevy Chase
    b. Brian-Doyle Murray
    c. Cleavon Little
    d. Gene Wilder

740) What is the name of Guardian Angel leader Curtis Silwa's wife who has taken up a part-time career in modeling?

. . . *Answers*

733. Stuttering

734. Roald Dahl

735. False (They're not married.)

736. Betty Friedan

737. Bill Graham

738. b

739. d

740. Lisa Silwa

741) What actress, famous for a chilling shower she once took, was discovered by Norma Shearer?

742) Who was named Admiral of the Ocean Seas and Viceroy and Governor General of all the islands he might discover, and also granted 1/10 of all the profits of his voyage:
   a. Balboa
   b. Columbus
   c. Magellan
   d. Drake

743) What actor, who had greatest fame on TV, became the father of triplets?

744) What tennis player has the nickname "Nasty"?

745) The famous marriage of Vivien Leigh and Laurence Olivier was the first for both stars. True or false?

746) Who is known as "The Mouth of The South"?

747) Who was responsible for the merger of the AFL and the CIO?

748) Who is the man behind the pig—the man who pulls the strings and speaks for Miss Piggy?

749) What young record producer became the lieutenant governor of California?

750) Author Peter Benchley (*Jaws*) is the third generation of Benchley writers. Name his famous literary father and grandfather.

. . . Answers

741. Janet Leigh (shower — *Psycho*)

742. b

743. Richard Thomas

744. Ilie Nastase

745. False (They both had spouses when they met.)

746. Ted Turner

747. George Meany

748. Frank Oz

749. Mike Curb

750. Father: Nathanial Benchley; grandfather: Robert Benchley

751) Sports announcer Howard Cosell was trained as a lawyer. True or false?

752) Frederick Remington was the inventor of the Remington rifle. True or false?

753) What high-flying Englishman was knighted for his efforts at ferrying people across the Atlantic Ocean?

754) Burt Reynolds created a sensation as the first male centerfold in what publication?

755) What daughter of a Mississippi carpenter is an opera star?

756) What do the initials "J.C." stand for in the famous retailer's name, J.C. Penney?

757) What well-known artist has been dubbed "the rich man's Norman Rockwell"?

758) Which of the following choreographers is best known for combining pop music with classical dance?
   a. George Balanchine
   b. Martha Graham
   c. Twyla Tharp
   d. Merce Cunningham

759) Among the current crop of actors, who is Jimmy Stewart's favorite?

760) What comedian was banned from the *Ed Sullivan Show* for allegedly making an obscene gesture at the show's host?

. . . Answers

751. True

752. False (He was a famous painter and sculptor of the American West.)

753. Freddie Laker

754. *Cosmopolitan*

755. Leontyne Price

756. James Cash

757. Andrew Wyeth

758. c

759. Dustin Hoffman

760. Jackie Mason

761) Who is the only actor in English history ever to be given the title of Lord?

762) Sarah Caldwell was the first female conductor of what opera company?

763) Representative Geraldine Ferraro is a three-term congresswoman from what borough of New York City?

764) TV actress Donna Dixon (*Bosom Buddies*) is married to what famous actor/comedian who used to be busy on Saturday nights?

765) What 5'9" tennis champion had the same size forearm as the late Rocky Marciano?

766) Who is the famous psychologist and author whose brother Jonas found the cure for polio?

767) Who beat Shirley Temple Black in a special election in 1967 for a seat in Congress?

768) Who was the first Russian defector to the U.S. who had been a star of the Bolshoi Ballet?
   a. Aleksandr Godunov
   b. Mikhail Baryshnikov
   c. Rudolf Nureyev
   d. Natalia Makarova

769) What Rolling Stones hit did Mick Jagger say he'd rather be dead than singing when he was forty years old?

. . . Answers

761. Lord Laurence Olivier

762. The New York Metropolitan Opera Company (The Met)

763. Queens

764. Dan Akroyd

765. Rod Laver (12" forearm)

766. Lee Salk

767. Pete McCloskey

768. a

769. "Satisfaction"

770) Jean Harris, convicted of second degree murder in the death of Dr. Herman Tarnower of Scarsdale Diet fame, was headmistress of what exclusive girl's school?

771) "Miss Lillian," President Carter's mother, once served with the Peace Corps in what country?

772) Angie Dickinson was once married to what well-known musician/composer?

773) What ballet great fathered a child with what Oscar-winning actress who is now linked with a famous playwright/actor. Name all three adults.

774) Which of the following was Rhodes Scholar?
   a. Congressman Jack Kemp
   b. Senator Gary Hart
   c. Rock Hudson
   d. Kris Kristofferson

775) Approximately how many months after her marriage to Stefano Casiraghi was Princess Caroline's healthy six-pound, ten-ounce baby born?

776) Who was the first woman to sue successfully for "palimony"?

777) Muhammed Ali, when he still went by the name Cassius Clay, cut a pop record. True or false?

778) Which of the following singers *isn't* an American Indian?
   a. Jimi Hendrix   c. Buffy Sainte-Marie
   b. Johnny Cash   d. Keith Moon

. . . *Answers*

770. The Madeira School

771. India

772. Burt Bacharach

773. Mikhail Baryshnikov (ballet), Jessica Lange (actress), Sam Shepard (actor/playwright)

774. d

775. Six months

776. Michelle Triola (Marvin)

777. True ("Stand By Me" in 1964)

778. d (Jimi Hendrix, incidentally, was ¼ Cherokee.)

779) Who is the President of France?

780) "Most porn films I've ever seen are a wonderful argument in favor of blindness." Who said it?
   a. Reverend Jerry Falwell
   b. critic Rex Reed
   c. publisher Al Goldstein
   d. singer Anita Bryant

781) Who is the film king of the Orient?

782) What was the President Andrew Jackson's nickname?

783) The Beatles and Steve Lawrence and Eydie Gorme were on a concert bill together. True or false?

784) Before he hit it big as a comedian, Rodney Dangerfield had to win both money and respect by selling aluminum siding. True or false?

785) What individual, famous for his malaprops, said, "That atomic bomb — it's dynamite!"
   a. Samuel Goldwyn
   b. Jimmy Durante
   c. Norm Crosby
   d. Archie Bunker

786) Who took over the Southern Christian Leadership Conference (SCLC) after the death of Reverend Martin Luther King?

787) Janet Guthrie was the first woman to qualify and take part in what prestigious racing car event?

. . . *Answers*

779. Francois Mitterand

780. c

781. Run Run Shaw

782. "Old Hickory"

783. True (Paramount Theater, N.Y.C., 1964)

784. True

785. a

786. Reverend Ralph Abernathy

787. Indianapolis 500

QUESTIONS

788) What present-day English movie star once said, "If I work fast enough, pack enough pictures in, I'll be a star before anyone realizes I'm not star material"?

789) Who is "Soul Brother Number One"?

790) The Berrigan brothers were priests active in the Vietnam antiwar movement. What were their first names?

791) John Derek "discovered" Ursula Andress. True or false?

792) Gabrielle Bonheur Chanel, the French fashion designer, was known by what other name?

793) What gangster coined the expression "G-men" to describe FBI agents?

794) Who was the first husband of Monaco's Princess Caroline?

795) Bob Guccione was an artist before he became the publisher of *Penthouse Magazine*. True or false?

796) What now-famous actress posed while an infant for an Ivory Snow advertisement?

797) What is former hostage Patty Hearst's husband's name?

798) Actor George Kennedy's first involvement with show business was when he was in the army, acting as technical advisor to what 1950s TV show?

. . . *Answers*

788. Michael Caine

789. James Brown

790. Daniel and Philip

791. False (He married her, but it was Marlon Brando who discovered her.)

792. "Coco"

793. Machine Gun Kelly

794. Phillipe Junot

795. True

796. Brooke Shields

797. Bernard Shaw

798. *You'll Never Get Rich* (also known as the *Sergeant Bilko Show*)

799) Before Erma Bombeck became a celebrity she lived in Centerville, Ohio across the street from what young radio personality who would soon become a major TV talk show host?

800) What son of a famous actor began his career in show business as the "Wonder Bread Boy"? (Hint: his brother is also a famous actor.)

801) Name the comedy team from which two highly respected film writer/directors emerged.

802) She played the bride of Frankenstein in the classic movie of the same name. But she also played the real-life bride to what legendary actor?

803) What famous silent-screen actor discovered Myrna Loy?

804) Which of the following celebrities named Jones wasn't born with that name?
   a. Spike Jones
   b. Shirley Jones
   c. Jennifer Jones
   d. James Earl Jones

805) Hawaiian singer Don Ho is Jewish. True or false?

806) Does Yul Brynner shave his head or is he bald?

807) What record label has Stevie Wonder worked for during his entire musical career?

. . . Answers

799. Phil Donahue

800. Eric Douglas (son of Kirk Douglas, brother of Michael Douglas)

801. Nichols and May (Mike Nichols and Elaine May)

802. Charles Laughton (His wife, the "Bride," was Elsa Lanchester.)

803. Rudolph Valentino

804. c (Phyllis Isley)

805. False

806. He shaves his head.

807. Motown

808) Who is the famous movie star who also acted as sewer commissioner of Provo Canyon, Utah?

809) What popular comedian grew up in his grandmother's bordello?

810) Asked on his deathbed if it was hard to die, who said, "Yes, but not as hard as doing comedy"?

811) What Texan writes enormously popular syndicated reviews of drive-in movies?

812) Who was the French minister of culture in 1963?

813) What daughter of a famous singer overcame anorexia nervosa and then wrote a book about her ordeal?

814) What was former First Lady "LadyBird" Johnson's maiden name?

815) John L. Lewis was:
   a. a boxer
   b. a labor leader
   c. a novelist
   d. none of the above

816) Authors William Cullen Bryant and Henry Wadsworth Longfellow were both descendants of what famous Mayflower settlers?

817) Washington Irving, the novelist, was named after George Washington. True or false?

. . . Answers

808. Robert Redford

809. Richard Pryor

810. Edmund Gwenn

811. Joe Bob Briggs

812. André Malraux

813. Cherry Boone O'Neill (daughter of Pat Boone)

814. Taylor

815. b

816. John and Priscilla Alden

817. True

818) What architect originated the glass house, designed the Chicago Federal Center, had a philosophy of "less is more," and produced plans that were the forerunner of the California ranch house?

819) Drew Pearson, famed Washington muckraking columnist, had a side business of selling a certain commodity which he advertised as "better than in the column." What did he sell?

820) Like China's Mao Tse-Tung, Ho Chi Minh composed poetry. True or false?

821) Joseph P. Kennedy outlived how many of his children?

822) Who was the leader of the provisional government of Russia immediately after the overthrow of the Czar in 1917?

823) Famed explorers Lewis and Clark began their expedition to the Pacific Ocean from what city?

824) Which of the following performed his or her greatest work before the age of sixty-five?
    a. Grandma Moses
    b. Guiseppe Verdi
    c. Winston Churchill
    d. Jean Renoir

825) What daughter of a U.S. president is a bestselling murder-mystery writer?

826) She was born in America, yet became the first woman member of the British Parliament. Who was she?

. . . *Answers*

818. Ludwig Mies Van Der Rohe

819. Manure

820. True

821. Four (Joseph Jr., Kathleen, John, and Robert)

822. Alexander Kerensky

823. St. Louis, Missouri

824. d

825. Margaret Truman

826. Lady Astor

827) The Rolling Stones hit song "Angie" is about the wife of what other rock star?

828) Which of the following show-biz celebrities was *not* a student of the Maharishi Mahesh Yogi?
   a. Donovan
   b. Mia Farrow
   c. Mick Jagger
   d. Bob Dylan

829) John Gregory Dunne was a famous 17th century poet. True or false?

830) What is Cher's real first name?

831) What was the name of the world champion boxer who had a sizzling love affair with French singer Edith Piaf?

832) TV personality Dennis James is the son of famed trumpeter Harry James. True or false?

833) What comedian has a legendary reputation for stealing jokes?

834) What singer/actress once had a well-publicized romance with comedian Steve Martin and costarred with him in two of his movies?

835) What rubber-faced American actor calls himself "The Ukrainian Cary Grant"?

836) Convicted murderer Gary Gilmore was executed in what state?

. . . *Answers*

827. David Bowie

828. d

829. False (John Donne is the poet. John Gregory Dunne is a present day novelist and screenwriter and husband of Joan Didion.)

830. Cherilyn

831. Marcel Cerdan

832. False

833. Milton Berle

834. Bernadette Peters

835. Walter Matthau

836. Utah

837) Actress Dixie Lee was the first wife of what famous singer?

838) Sissy is Sissy Spacek's real first name. True or false?

839) What is the name of Dolly Parton's rarely seen husband?

840) Helen Keller and Anne Sullivan performed an act on the vaudeville circuit. True or false?

841) What is the name of William Randolph Hearst's "palace" in California?

842) Famous brothers Chang and Eng (of mixed Chinese and Siamese ancestry) gave rise to what expression that has entered the English language?

843) Irving Berlin assigned the royalties to his song "God Bless America" to what two organizations?

844) How many years did it take James Joyce to write *Ulysses*?

845) What is the name of the woman who was with John Belushi when he died?

846) What legendary guitarist is married to the former wife of Beatle George Harrison?

847) What is Lord Snowdon's profession?

848) Dr. John S. Pemberton invented:
    a. pantyhose   c. Coca-Cola
    b. antidandruff shampoo   d. the first pinball machine

. . . Answers

837. Bing Crosby

838. False (It's Mary Elizabeth.)

839. Carl Dean

840. True (Between 1920 and 1924)

841. San Simeon

842. Siamese Twins

843. The Boy Scouts and Girl Scouts

844. Seven

845. Cathy Evelyn Smith

846. Eric Clapton (married to the former Patti Boyd Harrison)

847. Photography

848. c

849) What movie actress of the 1930s had her picture on Japanese-made condoms that were sold in America?

850) What ex-government investigator was caught in an attempt to "fix" the Neilsen ratings in 1966?

851) What star performers battled CBS in 1969 over censorship of their show, and lost?

852) The singing group The Isley Brothers aren't related to each other. True or false?

853) What talented Irish actor known for his philandering, drinking, and fighting had his nose broken at least eight times?

854) Which of the following is *not* a famous pollster?
    a. Elmo Roper
    b. Lawrence Harris
    c. Patrick Caddell
    d. George Gallup

855) Actor George Hamilton is actually George Hamilton IV. True or false?

856) What legendary sports figure was known as "Papa Bear"?

857) Who was the founder of the Gucci empire?

858) What comedian with a social conscience has been known to go on public fasts for causes he believes in?

. . . Answers

849. Sylvia Sidney

850. Rex Sparger

851. The Smothers Brothers

852. False (The original group were brothers; they've since added two more brothers and a cousin.)

853. Richard Harris

854. b (Louis Harris is the famous pollster.)

855. True

856. George Halas (long-time owner of the Chicago Bears football team)

857. Guccio Gucci (1906, in Florence, Italy)

858. Dick Gregory

859) Which of the following music personalities isn't Jewish?
   a. Linda Eastman
   b. Phoebe Snow
   c. Bruce Springsteen
   d. Phil Spector

860) Who has preached the Gospel to more millions than everyone else in history?

861) To some, he'll always be Sir Lancelot, but to Judy Garland he was "a living eight-by-ten glossy." Who was Judy referring to?

862) What bestselling modern poet was the co-founder of the famous City Lights Bookshop in San Francisco?

863) What singer performed "The Star-Spangled Banner" at a nationally televised World Series game in Ocotober, 1968 and ended his rendition with "hey, yeah!"?

864) What famous American writer went to prison rather than pay taxes which he claimed supported the institution of slavery?

865) In what country was labor leader James Hoffa born?

866) What did Yippie leader Abbie Hoffman and his wife Anita Kushner name their first child?

867) Herbert Khaury is the real name of what unusual singing star?

868) Which of the famous western outlaw Younger brothers committed suicide?

. . . *Answers*

859. c

860. Billy Graham

861. Robert Goulet (He played Sir Lancelot in the hit play, *Camelot*.)

862. Lawrence Ferlinghetti

863. José Feliciano

864. Henry David Thoreau

865. Brazil

866. "America"

867. Tiny Tim

868. James Younger

QUESTIONS

869) How many wives did Brigham Young have?

870) Before he made his name as a famous journalist/columnist, he sang in a trio that included George Jessel and worked in vaudeville for twelve years. At the end of his life he performed yet again as the narrator of a popular TV show. Who was he?

871) What famous Pulitzer Prize-winning poet was also a physician?

872) Who was the featured piano soloist at the premiere performance of George Gershwin's "Rhapsody in Blue"?

873) When asked about his interest in running for political office, what actor said, "I've played three presidents, three saints, and two geniuses. That should satisfy any man"?

874) Michelle Phillips was once married to what American actor/writer/director who rode to fame on the back of a motorcycle?

875) Who was the first black woman ever signed to a long-term Hollywood contract?

876) What was the name of the man who said he gave Howard Hughes a ride in the desert and later produced a will which indicated that he was an heir to the Howard Hughes fortune?

877) Multimillionaire Howard L. Hunt used to have his lunch flown to Texas every day from his favorite restaurant in Paris. True or false?

. . . Answers

869. Twenty-seven

870. Walter Winchell (He narrated *The Untouchables*.)

871. William Carlos Williams

872. George Gershwin

873. Charlton Heston

874. Dennis Hopper (*Easy Rider*)

875. Lena Horne

876. Melvin Dummar

877. False (He took his lunch to work in a brown paper bag.)

878) Mother Theresa won a Pulitzer Prize for her work for the poor of Calcutta, India. True or false?

879) Who is Meryl Streep's husband and what does he do for a living?

880) Actress Cheryl Ladd is the daughter of actor Alan Ladd. True or false?

881) Who made Elvis Presley wear a white tie and tails while singing "Hound Dog" to a pooch who was sitting on a stool?
   a. Ed Sullivan
   b. Steve Allen
   c. Jack Paar
   d. Howard Cosell

882) Who was the first baseball player to be paid $100,000 per year?

883) What famous photographer (long associated with the Sierra Club) is best known for capturing on film the beauty of landscapes and nature in such places as Yosemite Valley and the High Sierras?

884) Who was the first black man to have his name placed in nomination for vice president of a major political party?

885) What is the name of the Norwegian archeologist who sailed a primitive balsa wood raft from Peru to Polynesia in 1947?

886) Horatio Alger was a character in a series of children's books about hard work leading to success in the latter part of the 19th century. True or false?

. . . Answers

878. False (She won the Nobel Peace Prize.)

879. Donald Gummer. He's a sculptor.

880. False

881. b

882. Joe Di Maggio

883. Ansel Adams

884. Julian Bond (He withdrew his name because he was too young to run.)

885. Thor Heyerdahl (author of *Kon-Tiki*)

886. False (Horatio Alger was real. He wrote the books.)

887) Florence Nightingale Graham was the real name of what famous beauty specialist who built a cosmetic empire out of a $1,000 investment?

888) Who was the second man to walk on the moon?

889) Charles Atlas, before becoming the "World's Most Perfectly Developed Man," claims he had been a weakling, weighing how many pounds?

890) Fill in the missing name from these famous words spoken by Alexander Graham Bell: "Mr. _____ , come here; I want you."

891) What is Yogi Berra's real name?

892) Zanesville, Ohio is so named in honor of its most famous citizen, western writer Zane Grey. True or false?

893) Andrew Carnegie wrote *How to Win Friends and Influence People*. True or false?

894) What New York judge disappeared without a trace in 1930, creating a baffling mystery that remains unsolved to this day?

895) "Kid Blackie" was the name that a famous heavyweight boxer used when he began his career in 1914. What was this future champion's name?

896) Who was the first and only Supreme Court Justice forced to resign his seat?

. . . Answers

887. Elizabeth Arden

888. Edwin "Buzz" Aldrin

889. Ninety-seven ("A ninety-seven pound weakling")

890. Watson

891. Peter Lawrence Berra

892. False (Zane Grey was descended from the founder o Zanesville.)

893. False (*Dale* Carnegie wrote it.)

894. Judge Crater

895. Jack Dempsey

896. Abe Fortas

897) Actor Warner Oland, best known for his portrayal of Charlie Chan in sixteen movies, was actually:
   a. Hungarian
   b. German
   c. Swedish
   d. Norwegian

898) What two former presidents of the Screen Actors Guild went on to national political prominence?

899) What was the name of the famous playwright who was once married to actress Frances Farmer?

900) "Oh! Carol," the Neil Sedaka tune, was written about whom?

901) What famous black singer died because she was refused treatment in a Southern hospital, and whose death became the subject of a hit play by Edward Albee?

902) By what other name was the wealthy James Buchanan Brady known?

903) Who is taller, Wilt Chamberlain or Kareem Abdul-Jabbar?

904) Billy Joel's unusually shaped nose is due to:
   a. a career as an amateur boxer
   b. a football injury
   c. normal growth
   d. a motorcycle accident

905) Who is the director of the CIA?

. . . Answers

897. c

898. Senator George Murphy and President Ronald Reagan

899. Clifford Odets

900. Carole King

901. Bessie Smith (The play — *The Death of Bessie Smith*)

902. Diamond Jim Brady

903. Kareem Abdul-Jabbar (7'1⁵/₈" to Wilt's 7'1")

904. a (22 amateur bouts)

905. William Casey

906) What famous huge wrestler was hired to act as a double for Charles Laughton during the filming of *Henry the Eighth*?

907) What TV comic made the expression "Well, I'll be a dirty bird" popular in the 1950s?

908) Who was discovered as a model by Diana Vreeland and then discovered as a movie star by "Slim" and Howard Hawks?

909) Czar Ivan the Terrible was so "terrible" that in an angry fit he killed his own son, Ivan. True or false?

910) Movie tough guy George Raft got his start in show business as:
    a. a stuntman
    b. a nightclub dancer
    c. a dialogue coach
    d. a bodyguard for Jack L. Warner

911) Who took down *Mein Kampf* from Hitler's dictation and served as his secretary and bodyguard?

912) Antoine De La Mothe Cadillac was the founder of Detroit. True or false?

913) Robert Truax is a private citizen in Saratoga, California who is building something very unusual in his backyard. What is he building?

914) What singer became despondent over the death of Freddie Prinze, quit show business, and then made a big comeback?

. . . Answers

906. Man Mountain Dean

907. George Gobel

908. Lauren Bacall

909. True

910. b

911. Rudolf Hess

912. True

913. A space ship

914. Tony Orlando

915) Bob Hope said the following about the Reagans: "Ronnie's hero is Calvin Coolidge and Nancy's is Calvin _____."

916) *Washington Post* Executive Editor Ben Bradlee is married to what well-known news personality?

917) Who is Joan Collins' sister who is a bestselling writer?

918) Actress Virginia Mayo's father invented mayonnaise. True or false?

919) MGM's boy-genius, Irving Thalberg, married which of his studio's stars?

920) Who was Hollywood's "Oomph girl"?

921) Jeannette MacDonald and Nelson Eddy were husband and wife. True or false?

922) Although Anthony Quinn is best known as Zorba the Greek, he isn't Greek. He's Anthony the _____.

923) Before marrying Clark Gable, Carol Lombard married a Powell. But which one: Dick Powell or William Powell?

924) Who often played British butlers in films and played sidekick to Merv Griffin?

925) What blond pop singer/actress opened a boutique called "Koalo Blue" in L.A. which features clothes designed exclusively by Australians?

. . . *Answers*

915. Klein

916. Sally Quinn

917. Jackie Collins

918. False

919. Norma Shearer

920. Ann Sheridan

921. False

922. Mexican

923. William Powell

924. Arthur Treacher

925. Olivia Newton-John (She's Australian.)

926) The first movie in which Frank Stallone's music was heard was one his brother Sylvester directed, *Staying Alive*. True or false?

927) Queen Beatrix is the reigning monarch of what European country?

928) What tavern in New York City (that is *still* in business) was the site of General George Washington's farewell dinner to his officers at the end of the Revolutionary War?

929) After her relationship with Nicky Arnstein, Fanny Brice married what well-known showman?

930) *Heart Like A Wheel*, starring Bonnie Bedelia, is a movie about what real-life female race car driver?

931) "Miss Vickie," Tiny Tim's ex-wife, is now the weather forecaster on an L.A. TV news program. True or false?

932) Who is the TV actor brother of comedienne Mary Gross?

933) Alexandre Gustave Eiffel, of Eiffel Tower fame, engineered the iron structure of what famous American monument?

934) What Communist (who would later become famous) worked in his youth as a cook's helper in London for the world-renowned master chef, Escoffier?

935) Who was the movie director svengali behind the film career of Cybil Shepherd?

. . . Answers

926. False (He wrote music for four other films before *Staying Alive*, including *Rocky I, II, and III.*)

927. The Netherlands

928. Fraunces Tavern

929. Billy Rose

930. Shirley Muldowney

931. False

932. Michael Gross (of *Family Ties*)

933. The Statue of Liberty

934. Ho Chi Minh

935. Peter Bogdonavich

936) What comedian built his routines (and his reputation) on the daily newspaper he would brandish during his act?

937) Actor/director John Cassevetes is married to what actress who stars in many of his movies?

938) Buddy Rogers is best known as:
   a. a drummer
   b. husband of Mary Pickford
   c. children's TV star, Mr. Rogers
   d. none of the above

939) What department store heir is responsible for raising a three-ton safe from the underwater wreckage of the *Andrea Doria*?

940) What famous humanitarian financed his medical work by giving organ recitals in Europe?

941) Al, Jim and Harry were the three brothers who made up what popular comedy team?

942) Sally Rand was the author of *Atlas Shrugged*. True or false?

943) Charlie Chaplin's wife Oona is the daughter of what famous playwright who was adamantly against their marriage?

944) What famous actor, who has refused to endorse any products, has recently come out with his own spaghetti sauce?

945) Congressman Wayne Hays had an affair with a "secretary" he hired who couldn't type. She later did a nude pictorial for *Playboy Magazine*. What is her name?

. . . *Answers*

936. Mort Sahl

937. Gena Rowlands

938. b

939. Peter Gimbel

940. Dr. Albert Schweitzer

941. The Ritz Brothers

942. False (Sally Rand was a striptease fan dancer. *Ayn* Rand wrote *Atlas Shrugged*.)

943. Eugene O'Neill

944. Paul Newman ("Newman's Own")

945. Elizabeth Ray

946) Dance studio mogul Arthur Murray appeared in several MGM movie musicals. True or false?

947) Name the two actress daughters of John Mills.

948) In the 1870s photographer Eadweard Muybridge proved with the aid of a camera that a trotting horse always has at least one foot on the ground. True or false?

949) Riccardo Muti became the conductor of the Philadelphia Orchestra after whose forty-four year reign?

950) "I've put in so many enigmas and puzzles that it will keep the professors busy for centuries arguing over what I meant, and that's the only way of ensuring one's immortality." What writer said it?
   a. Marcel Proust
   b. Franz Kafka
   c. James Joyce
   d. Philip Roth

951) Actor Eric Roberts (*The Pope of Greenwich Village*) is engaged in a long term relationship with what actress?

952) What is the name of the French artist who created pointillism (small dots of pure color that blend when seen from a distance) and about whom a new Broadway musical has been produced?

953) The International Monetary Fund (IMF) was established in 1944 to keep order in the world's monetary system. What is the name of the brilliant British economist behind its creation?

. . . Answers

946. False

947. Hayley and Juliet Mills

948. False (He proved that a trotting horse sometimes has all four feet *off* the ground.)

949. Eugene Ormandy

950. c

951. Sandy Dennis

952. Georges Seurat (The Broadway musical — *Sunday In The Park With George*)

953. John Maynard Keynes

954) What is the name of the American who was captured when his plane went down over Syrian-held Lebanon?

955) Walter Matasschanskayasky is the real name of Walter Matthau. True or false?

956) Who was Britain's Jewish prime minister?

957) "The Little Sparrow" was the nickname of what performer?

958) Lord Snowdon and Lord Lichfield each vied to become the official photographer of Prince Charles and Lady Diana's wedding. Who was the victor?

959) Ernie Barnes is the name of the former football player for the San Diego Chargers and Denver Broncos who did all the paintings for what character on what TV situation comedy?

960) Jean Simmons married Farley Granger. True or false?

961) Country western singer Jessi Colter is married to which of the following country western stars?
    a. Merle Haggard   c. Roger Miller
    b. Waylon Jennings   d. Willie Nelson

962) Supervisor Dan White of San Francisco shot and killed what two San Francisco city officials?

963) The recent Disney film *Never Cry Wolf* (starring Charles Martin Smith) was adapted from what real-life individual's 1963 account of his time in the North among wolves?

. . . Answers

954. Robert Goodman

955. False (For years he claimed it was his real name but, in fact, his real name is Walter Matthow.)

956. Benjamin Disraeli

957. Edith Piaf

958. Lord Lichfield

959. "J.J." on *Good Times*

960. False (She married Stewart Granger.)

961. b

962. George Moscone (Mayor) and Harvey Milk (Supervisor)

963. Farley Mowat

964) Who was the last surviving signer of the Mayflower compact?

965) Jerry Lewis has a son who made it big for a while in rock 'n roll. What was the full name of his son's group?

966) By what nickname was Rose Kennedy's father known?

967) What was the name of the judge who presided over the famous trial of the "Chicago Seven"?

968) What is the name of Pat Boone's wife?

969) Which of the following is true about Lizzie Borden?
   a. she was thirty-two when her parents "passed away"
   b. there was a total of nineteen "whacks"
   c. she was acquitted and collected her inheritance
   d. all of the above

970) David Stockman is the "boy wonder" director of what U.S. government office?

971) Who was the American writer responsible for "inventing" the modern detective story?

972) What actor (who has since become a movie sex symbol) had a small role on the cast of recording of the Broadway musical *Over There*, starring the Andrews Sisters?

973) How did Francis Stanley (of "Stanley Steamer" car fame) die?

974) John B. Stetson, creator of the men's cowboy hat known as a "Stetson," started his business in what city?

. . . Answers

964. John Alden

965. Gary Lewis and The Playboys

966. "Honey Fitz"

967. Judge (Julius J.) Hoffman

968. Shirley

969. d

970. Office of Management and Budget (OMB)

971. Edgar Allan Poe

972. John Travolta

973. In an automobile accident

974. Philadelphia

975) What NBC newsman is especially well known as a nit-picker about the proper use of the English language?

976) What visionary inventor attempted wireless communication with other planets at the end of the 19th century?

977) What U.S. Senator married two different Miss South Carolinas?

978) Louis Comfort Tiffany, the creator of Tiffany lamps, was the son of the founder of Tiffany's, the famous jewelry company. True or false?

979) Who was America's first "crooner"?

980) What owner of the Cleveland Indians baseball team was responsible for hiring a midget to pinch-hit against opposing pitchers?

981) Who was the only Confederate naval commander to sail the "Stars and Bars" around the world?

982) What famous New York City mayor wrote the hit song, "Will You Love Me In December As You Do In May?"

983) What does the "C" in Alabama Governor George C. Wallace's name stand for?

984) Montgomery Ward was actually two people, James Montgomery and Christopher Ward. True or false?

985) Frederick Weyerhaueser was known as:
    a. The Lingerie King   c. The Candy King
    b. The Lumber King   d. The Wire King

. . . Answers

975. Edwin Newman

976. Nikola Tesla

977. Strom Thurmond

978. True

979. Rudy Vallee

980. Bill Veeck

981. James Waddell

982. Jimmy Walker

983. Corley

984. False

985. b

986) What well-known music personality is the father of an adopted son named Hans Christian Henderson?

987) *Stag Party* was the original name of what famous publisher's magazine?

988) What housewife became a famous comedienne after being discovered on the Groucho Marx TV show, *You Bet Your Life*?

989) What female film superstar, who got her big break as a regular on a popular TV comedy show, once earned her living as a go-go dancer?

990) What is the name of actor Rex Harrison's son, who starred in a modestly popular TV show during the late 1960s?

991) What famous movie producer, on the occasion of his 100th birthday, attributed his longevity to the fact that he had given up cigarettes two year before?

992) What first name was Nipsy Russell given at birth?

993) Who won the Senate seat left vacant by the death of Joseph R. McCarthy?

994) What football star is the son of blind parents?

995) What was the name of the successful family that built automobiles in the 20th century and was also the largest manufacturer of horse-drawn wagons in the 19th century?

996) What famous Irish actor *always* wears emerald-green socks?

. . . Answers

986. Skitch Henderson

987. *Playboy Magazine* (Hugh Hefner, publisher, changed it when *Stag Magazine* objected.)

988. Phyllis Diller

989. Goldie Hawn (the show was *Rowan and Martin's Laugh-in.*)

990. Noel Harrison (*The Girl From U.N.C.L.E.*)

991. Adolph Zukor

992. Nipsy (It's his real name.)

993. William Proxmire

994. Jim Plunkett

995. Studebaker

996. Peter O'Toole

997) With whom is singer Diahann Carrol romantically linked?

998) What famous singer/actress was born in Hawaii and was an extra in the 1966 movie *Hawaii*?

999) Whom does Frank Sinatra credit for everything he knows about musical phrasing?

1000) What Academy Award-winning actor has a lifetime disability pension for a wound he received near his spine during World War II?

1001) What lawyer argued for the NAACP in the famous 1954 Supreme Court desegragation case, Brown vs. Topeka, Kansas Board of Education?

1002) What country western singing star became a grandmother at age thirty-one?

1003) Who received the last telephone call Marilyn Monroe made before she died?

1004) Lorna Luft's parents collaborated on only one movie. What was it?

1005) Actress Estelle Parsons's first boyfriend when she was a teenager ultimately became what movie star?

. . . Answers

997. Vic Damone

998. Bette Midler

999. Singer Mabel Mercer

1000. Lee Marvin

1001. Thurgood Marshall (who later became the first black Supreme Court Justice of the U.S.)

1002. Loretta Lynn

1003. Peter Lawford

1004. *A Star Is Born* (Sid Luft as producer and Judy Garland as star)

1005. Jack Lemmon